Child Poverty

Neriman Aral / Figen Gürsoy / Ece Özdoğan Özbal /
Saliha Çetin Sultanoğlu / Sebahat Aydos / Selim Tosun /
Tuğba Karaaslan / Gül Kadan

Child Poverty

PL ACADEMIC
RESEARCH

Bibliographic Information published by the Deutsche Nationalbibliothek
The Deutsche Nationalbibliothek lists this publication in the Deutsche
Nationalbibliografie; detailed bibliographic data is available in the internet
at http://dnb.d-nb.de.

Library of Congress Cataloging-in-Publication Data
Names: Aral, Neriman, author.
Title: Child poverty / Neriman Aral [and seven others].
Description: Frankfurt am Main ; New York : Peter Lang, [2017] |
Includes bibliographical references.
Identifiers: LCCN 2016052571 | ISBN 9783631698402
Subjects: LCSH: Children—Turkey—Ankara—Social conditions. | Children—Turkey—
Ankara—Economic conditions. | Poor children—Turkey—Ankara. | Poverty—Turkey—
Ankara. | Child welfare—Turkey—Ankara.
Classification: LCC HQ792.T9 A725 2017 | DDC 305.2309563/6—dc23 LC record
available at https://lccn.loc.gov/2016052571

This book has been prepared under the Project named "Mapping of Mamak District Child
Poverty" that is supported by T.C. Ankara Development Agency and has the code of
TR51/14/SOSKA/0041. All responsibility of the content belongs to Ankara University and
content does not reflect T.C. Ankara Development Agency's views.

ISBN 978-3-631-69840-2 (Print)
E-ISBN 978-3-631-69841-9 (E-PDF)
E-ISBN 978-3-631-69842-6 (EPUB)
E-ISBN 978-3-631-69843-3 (MOBI)
DOI 10.3726/b10711

Foreword

Socio-economic causes such as unemployment, migration and illiteracy underlie the problem of child poverty. Child poverty significantly impacts children's future and is a critical obstacle in the development of education and life standards. Growing up in poverty results in unfavorable outcomes in child development. Children's education can be hindered while poverty leads to malnutrition and illness. Research on poverty does not only deal with the financial perspective, it also examines the social, cultural and emotional perspectives. The most effective way of preventing child poverty is educating and improving the social skills of both children and parents, and raising awareness on children's rights. In this context, the children and the youth, who play the greatest role in the development of the country, should be supported and prepared for the future. Therefore, policymakers and researchers are tasked with a great responsibility to ensure the children and the youth do not face the threat of poverty.

Investigation of child poverty is necessary for raising awareness on the subject. Therefore, both physical and emotional development of children living in disadvantaged neighborhoods should be supported and their access to basic needs should be facilitated. In view of this perspective, an action plan was developed to characterize the poverty experienced by the children living in the Mamak district, to support their development, to discuss the extent of their victimhood and to generate solutions. Mamak is a metropolitan district of Ankara and 587.565 people live in Mamak according 2014 data. Mamak is an important residential area of Ankara, which has a population of approximately five million. In addition, one of the reasons for choosing Mamak as the project area was the fact that it is one of the foremost migration-receiving districts of Ankara.

In line with the project goals, the following activities were planned: Determining the poverty rate in Mamak, identifying the causes of child poverty in Mamak, mapping and reporting child poverty in Mamak, conducting a survey for 300 participants, interviewing 20 residents, organizing a workshop with the participation of the stakeholders for the presentation of the study data, developing an action plan for the prevention of child poverty in Mamak, building a project website, constructing a sample study model for researchers, and resuming efforts in other provinces after the completion of the project.

This study was carried out in a three-month period between February 05 and May 05, 2016 within the scope of Ankara Development Agency Direct Activity Support.

In the study, a questionnaire was developed as the data collection tool by the project team after conducting a review of literature, consultations with specialists, and pilot schemes in order to characterize household living and poverty conditions. The questionnaire was administered to 408 parents at their places of residence. In addition, in-depth knowledge of child poverty was also needed for its prevention in the district. Therefore, interviews were conducted to identify the opinions of the local residents on child poverty and to obtain their subjective assessments. 20 parents and 20 children were individually interviewed to characterize the perspectives of both the parents and the children. A workshop was organized with the participation of the people residing in Mamak and those who could contribute to the district on April 15, 2016 to support the study data. An action plan was developed according to the study data and the information obtained from the workshop.

Albeit their low educational attainment, the parents interviewed wanted their children to receive education and find decent employment. As a result, the children had a high rate of school attendance. The majority of the children began elementary school on time and continued to attend school throughout compulsory education. Although approximately half of the parents stated that they had difficulty in covering school expenses and the majority said that they could spare 100 TL per month for their children's education, the majority of the families received moral and material support for their children's educational needs. However, half of the families said that their children's school attendance was hindered due to poverty.

The parents and the children were queried on what they wanted to change about themselves. The parents said that they wanted a decent job and a better education, a happy marriage, a prosperous life, while the children said they wanted to live elsewhere, not be poor and receive a better education. Furthermore, the children expressed that they wanted people to behave better toward others, an end to terror and wars, and equality for all.

In view of the knowledge gained from the workshop carried out with the participation of the residents and numerous specialists working in the field or employed at institutions relevant to child poverty, an action plan was developed, short- and long-term actions were agreed upon, and the institutions and organizations responsible for action were suggested.

We would like to express our eternal gratitude to Ankara Development Agency who contributed to the realization of the study, Ankara University who we are proud of being a member, the District Governorate of Mamak who contributed to our interviews with parents and children, Mamak Social Assistance and Solidarity Foundation, the District National Education Directorate of Mamak, and the parents and children residing in Mamak who opened their doors to the project team for the collection of the study data. We hope the study provides guidance to researchers and policymakers.

Prof. Dr. Neriman Aral

AUTHORS

Prof. Dr. Neriman Aral

Prof. Dr. Figen Gürsoy

Expert Ece Özdoğan Özbal

Res. Assist. Saliha Çetin Sultanoğlu

Expert Sebahat Aydos

Res. Assist. Selim Tosun

Dr. Tuğba Karaaslan

Instructor Gül Kadan

Contents

Appendix List

List of Tables

17

List of Figures

1. Introduction

Even though there is not any definition agreed on by everyone, poverty can be expressed as the inability to meet basic needs required by the minimum living standard. Results obtained from researches indicate that poverty has been a problem that must be solved not only for the developing countries but also for the developed countries which have a relatively high share of social spending.

Lack of fair distribution of resources, overpopulation, lack of educational and employment opportunities, some economic and demographic trends, factors such as rapid degradation of the environment are among the main factors causing poverty. Lack of social assistance is also among the causes of poverty (Ceren, 2013). Whatever the reason behind it, poverty, in almost every country of the world, has become a serious problem having economic, social and psychological dimensions (ASAGEM, 2010). Today, all societies in the globalized world have been trying to fight against poverty.

Poverty is an issue that should be examined through various layers of the society. Negative effects of poverty have been felt more especially by the people with special needs such as the elderly who are exposed to different type of vulnerabilities and disabilities, women, and children in both developed and developing countries (Durgun, 2011; UNDP, 2014). Poverty especially affects children's lives and health and there is an inverse ratio between educational level and poverty (Kaya, 2011; Wang, 2015). In the future, the chance the children that will become adult members of a society can vary depending on whether their country is rich or poor, whether they were born in a poor or wealthy family and whether they live in the rural or urban areas.

A significant portion of the approximately 18,000 children who lose their lives every day around the globe, cannot reach services for reasons such as poverty, geographical location, and this number mainly consists of children living in neighborhoods in the urban or rural areas. Though they can be easily rescued with very low cost treatments, such as diarrhea which can be effectively and cheaply treated by oral saline supplementation, children continue to die everyday. A child born into a wealthy family has four times higher chance to benefit from this therapy compared to a child of the poor family (UNICEF, 2013).

21

In the "World Children's Status Report 2005" there is a definition of necessary material, immaterial and emotional sources required in terms of the poverty of children: "Children living in poverty, are living deprived survival, growth and development and thus they cannot benefit from their rights, cannot fully develop their potential and cannot participate in the society as full and equal members of the society" (UNICEF, 2005). It is seen in research that; homeless people face poverty (Sharam & Hulse, 2014), women especially encounter not only materialistic but also social dimensions of poverty in a negative way (Aktaş, 2013; Yusufoğlu & Kızmaz, 2015), children in poor families live deprived of their rights, experience health problems and are forced to work (Öztürk, 2008).

The inequality children are exposed to and the consequences of it have been contradictory to the principles accepted in the Convention on the Rights of the Child (CRC). These principles are not to discriminate (Article 2), the child's best interests must be a primary concern (Article 3), children have right to live and to survive (Article 6), and respect to children's views (Article 12). In the principles located at the core of the CRC which give meaning to the struggle with poverty as a problem for all societies, it is emphasized that whatever their race, color, sex, religion, language and political or any another kind of opinion are, all children have rights in all decisions affecting children, their interest should be considered and their life, survival and the development in order to achieve the full potential of children and to express their views freely on the subjects affecting them, and they have rights ensuring these views are taken seriously.

Child poverty affects millions of children's lives worldwide. It's not just in poor countries, this situation seen in rich countries increase the probability of uneducated, poor, undernourished children to be uneducated, malnourished, poor adults in the future (UNDP, 2004). It stated in a survey that people who experienced poverty in childhood, have poor memory, are slow in speaking and have more depression in adulthood (Tampubolan, 2016). Neurobiological research shows that drawbacks experienced in early childhood continue to affect in adulthood. Diseases and malnutrition in the early stages can negatively affect the learning abilities of children and thereby the chance to make their living (UNICEF, 2014). Researches also show that the probability of in poor child fatality families is higher than in families with a good financial situation, and children of poor families are hospitalized due to the preventable diseases more than other children (Eryurt & Koç, 2009; Lessard et al., 2012). Similarly, according to the results of a survey examining the environmental risk factors for the development of children, it is noteworthy that as the number of risk factors increases, deviation in the development can be seen, or they are more likely to have delays in development. Factors such as other's mental illness, anxious mother, mother who has inappropriate value and beliefs to grow a child, mother exhibiting negative attitudes towards children and if there is no relationship between early infant and mother, the absence of a identified profession of parents, low education level of the mother, father who does not live with the family, experiencing stressful events within the first four years, and parents having four or more children are environmental risk factors that are reported to have adverse affects on children's cognitive development (Sameroff, 1993; Wei et al., 2015). Risk factors on poverty are also important.

A closer look at the lives of low-income families living in poverty will provide a better understanding in terms of the impact of poverty on families and children. Poverty-related chronic high-stress levels can harm the physical and mental health of the parents and can cause high levels of stress-related medical conditions (hypertension, asthma, etc.) and psychological problems (depression, anxiety, troubled relationships, substance abuse, etc.) (Frieberg et al., 2015; Özmen et al., 2008; Santiego et al. 2013; Datta & Singh, 2015). Sources of the stress that occur in parallel with poverty can also affect parent's ability to provide sensitive and compassionate care which is essential for maximizing brain development and which has lifelong effects (Zuckerman & Sandel, 2013). It is seen in researches that the brain growth in infancy and early childhood period of children from low socio-economic level evolves more slowly and factors such as parenting styles and family history affect brain growth (Hanson et al., 2013; Dickerson & Papli, 2015).

Children exposed to the above listed environmental risk factors, frequently encountered in poor families, in their early childhood and children who cannot receive compassionate care will not receive the training that is required for their optimal development in their older ages and furthermore, can be forced to work in poor conditions threatening their health and safety in order to contribute to their families (Bilgin, 2009; Koyun & Çiçekoğlu, 2011; Aung, 2015). A child providing temporary contribution to his/her family, will soon have to begin working consistently over time due to his contribution to family's income. Children who enter the workforce at an early age at a job with conditions that threaten their health and safety, and children who work for very low wages in comparison with their labor in poor conditions, have difficulties in continuing education. Millions of children around the world are reported to have been working in order to provide more monetary contribution to their families in jobs disrupting their education, preventing them to live their childhood and interrupting their optimal physical and mental development (Durgun, 2011; UNICEF, 2014).

Child poverty is very important for the development of children, development and improvement of the society. Every step will be taken towards the resolution of child poverty that can prevent the withdrawal of the children from the employment that necessitates more education in the developing world and is crucially important in the rapidly changing world for more productive future generations (Durgun, 2011). It is seen in a research, poor children enter the marginalized communities especially in rural areas and they cannot eat healthily nor continue their education (Dornan & Pells, 2015). Taking the necessary measures on child poverty is also important in terms of preventing a society that will live in poverty.

It is important to determine the current status of the process in the prevention of child poverty. Determining the status by obtaining scientific data based on evidence of a problem is the most important stage since it will reveal the source(s) of the problem. The data will form the basis for decisions and provide evidence for the assessment done and to-do. Data on children's and their families' poverty should be determined in a sustainable way, and necessary measures should be updated and improved in this direction.

According to "The State of the World's Children Report" published in January 2014 by UNICEF, data shows that progress has been achieved in the fight against poverty, but also reveals that the inequalities in children's conditions still exist. With the data, those who are at risk the most are determined, in other words, children who are least visible and most remote of the community are determined. Every society should identify the most remote individuals and children who are in need and should look for ways to meet their requirements, in order for them to develop (UNICEF, 2014).

In line with this reason, we have aimed to map child poverty in Mamak district in Ankara to support both spiritual and physical development of children who live in disadvantaged areas and to mediate them to achieve basic needs, to discuss the size of the grievance, and the preparation of the action plan for the production of solutions.

It is expected that revealing the source of the problem by identifying child poverty in Mamak district with a descriptive survey model on a regional basis will set the ground for preparing necessary action plans, taking the local conditions into consideration.

2. Method

Based on the description of the state of child poverty in Mamak, district of Ankara, and on the described conditions, first the research model, population and sample and the study group were explained and then the information in regard to the development of the data collection tools, data collection, analysis and interpretation were given in the method part of the research that was conducted in order to offer suggestions about what would be done to prevent child poverty in the region.

2.1. Research Model

In the research that was made to conduct studies to prevent the child poverty based on the description of the state of child poverty in Mamak and the condition described, it is aimed to reveal the general conditions of the households and the conditions of the house/living quarters and the children. In line with this objective, since the condition was attempted to be analyzed and examined in detail in terms of the scope and method, a mixed model, in which quantitative and qualitative research models are used together, was used. The quantitative data was obtained with the use of the descriptive survey model in the research. Survey models are suitable for the researches that aim to describe a past or a current condition as it was/is present (Karasar, 1999).

Within the scope of the research, in order to prevent the child poverty in the research, detailed information in regard to the child poverty is needed. Thus, interviews were conducted to reveal the opinions of the persons in the region about child poverty and to receive their subjective evaluations within the scope of the study. In the research that was planned to determine the child poverty, individual face-to-face interviews were made both with families and children to reveal both the family and child aspect.

To support the quantitative and qualitative data, a workshop, in which the people living in Mamak region and likely to contribute to that region ensured participation, was performed. Within the workshop, an action plan that would be applied as an output in the region was formed.

2.2. Universe, Sample and Study Group

The research population is composed of about 60000 people who applied to Mamak Social Assistance and Solidarity Foundation in Mamak District Governorship for social assistance support or took advantage of this support. It is understood in the interviews conducted with Mamak Social Assistance and Solidarity Foundation that there were about 10000 active files registered. Registered active file means that a benefit period of these people is continuing. Since the entire population cannot be reached due to time and opportunity limitations, sampling was taken from the population. From the purposeful sampling methods, criterion sampling was used for the sampling selection. Criterion sampling refers to selecting those who are within the scope of the sampling in accordance with a criterion (Yıldırım & Şimşek, 2005). Sampling criterion involves the people selected from those who applied to Mamak Social Assistance and Solidarity Foundation in Mamak District Governorship to utilize social assistance support or utilized this support. In regard to determining the sampling number, it was determined as seen in Table 3.1 considering the confidence level of 95% and the error margin of 5%.

Table 2.1. Sample Sizes For Two Different Confidence Level and Various Precision Limits (Yazıcıoğlu & Erdoğan, 2004)

Size of Universe	Precision (Condoned Fault)				
	±1%	±2%	±3%	±4%	±5%
1.000	**	**	**	375	278
2.000	**	**	696	462	322
3.000	**	1334	787	500	341
4.000	**	1500	842	522	350
5.000	**	1622	879	536	357
10.000	4899	1936	964	566	370
20.000	6489	2144	1013	583	377
50.000	8057	2291	1045	593	381
100.000	8763	2345	1056	597	383
500.000–∞	9423	2390	1065	600	384

As seen in Table 2.1, considering the application records of 60000 people, the sampling should be a minimum of 383 people. 300 people subscribed within the scope of the sampling in the project, however, it was decided that sampling should be at least 383 people upon determining the exact number of the population in the project process. 383 parents were determined within the scope of the research. However, the project team reached 408 parents. In this regard, 408 parents attending the study were accepted as the sampling.

A study group was determined to collect the qualitative data. In the study group, interviews were done with parents and children. It was paid attention that as in the criterion sampling, the people were selected from those who applied to Mamak Social Assistance and Solidarity Foundation for social assistance support or utilized this support and from their children. In this scope, 20 parents who accepted voluntary participation in the study, received social assistance support from the Social Assistance and Solidarity Foundation, applied and have children were interviewed. Moreover, interviews were also conducted with 20 children within the scope of the research.

Within the scope of the research, the study group of the workshop that was formed to support the quantitative and qualitative data is composed of 50 people. Within the scope of workshop, seven academicians from Ankara University, an academician from Çankırı Karatekin University, an academician from Hacettepe University, four school administrators and 12 teachers from Mamak District, a social worker and a psychologist from Mamak Social Assistance and Solidarity Foundation, an assistant expert from Ankara Migration Provincial Migration Management, two experts from KIZILAY, a social worker from Ministry of Family and Social Policy General Director of Child Services, a child development expert from Family and Social Policy General Director of Child Services General Director of Disabled and Elderly Services, a child development expert from Child Development Foundation, a social worker from Mamak Social Assistance and Solidarity Foundation, two podiatrists from developmental pediatrics association, two experts from Ankara Development Agency, three workers from Mamak Municipality, two reeves and two members from Mamak District, three people in charge and three pre-school teachers from Ankara University joined the workshop.

2.3. Ethics of Study

Before applying the research, interviews with Mamak District Governorship were completed and correspondences about collaboration were done in

January 2016. Parents who answered the questionnaires were informed of the content of the questionnaire before answering the questionnaire. Prior to the interview, the parents interviewed were informed and their written consent were taken. Children were also informed and the parents provided their written consent and attention was paid to the voluntary participation. Those who did not continue the questionnaire or the interview were not forced to do so and the data of these participants were excluded from the evaluation.

2.4. Data Collection Tools

Descriptive research data of the research was collected with the questionnaire (Appendix-1) formed by the researchers for the research while the data to be collected through the qualitative interviews of the research was collected with the semi-structured interview form (Appendix-2) again formed by the researchers.

To prepare a "Questionnaire on Mapping the Child Poverty in Mamak", a literature review about the issue was conducted. Poverty criteria, poverty criteria aspects and their reflections on daily life in the literature were examined in detail. In light of the information obtained, the draft questionnaire formed on 22nd January 2016 was shared with all the researchers in the project team. In line with the opinions and suggestions of seven people in the research team about the draft questionnaire, an update of the questionnaire was done on 2nd February 2016. The project team came together on 8th February 2016 and completed the last review of the questionnaire. The questionnaire in its final form was presented to two academic members working in the field of assessment and evaluation and changes were made in accordance with the suggestions. Its pilot application was applied to 20 people on 9th February 2016 and the "Questionnaire on Mapping the Child Poverty in Mamak" in Appendix 1 was put into its final form.

To perform the interviews constituting the qualitative aspect of the research, draft interview questions were formed by the project team. The interview questions were sent to the experts from the project team and from the assessment and evaluation and experts conducting studies on the field of poverty on 23rd February 2016. The questions in the interview form that was arranged after the expert opinions were applied to three mothers and two children out of the study group and thus, its pilot application was performed. The semi-structured interview form was put into its final form after the application (Appendix-2).

The questions (Appendix-3) indented to be evaluated in the workshop formed to support quantitative and qualitative research data were prepared by receiving the opinions of the experts in the research team. The questions formed of four open-ended questions were used respectively. Besides, forms were prepared to perform SWOT analysis in the workshop (Appendix-4).

2.5. Data Collection Method

In the data collection process, the studies were sustained in collaboration with Mamak Social Assistance and Solidarity Foundation. The process starting with creating a file after the application of the person in regard to the social assistance provided by Mamak Social Assistance and Solidarity Foundation continues with the house investigation made by the Foundation personnel. The social survey reports written as a result of the house investigation are evaluated in the weekly meetings of the board of trustees. Also considering the house income and opinions of the personnel visiting there for investigation, a decision on whether the relevant house is in need of help is given by the board.

The research team, accordingly, collected the data with the questionnaire by interviewing first with the people who applied to Mamak Social Assistance and Solidarity Foundation or receive social assistance from the foundation. However, since collecting data only from the people coming to the foundation is not sufficient in terms of observing the living environment of the people and its diversity, data was collected also by visiting the houses visited by the foundation personnel for house investigation. House visits were performed within the knowledge and planning of the foundation personnel.

On the first day of the house visits, a region visit was made with the foundation personnel. In this way, it is ensured that the researchers gave confidence to the participants. During the data collection process, participants frequently told the researchers that as they saw them with the foundation team they confidentially received them into their house. Sometimes, some of the research team members were called and asked whether other researchers going around the research were from the team or not.

The participants in expectation of assistance answered the questionnaire voluntarily in the data collection process. In the questionnaire data collection, generally the questions were asked by the researchers and the answers given by the participants were marked in the questionnaire by the researcher. The data was collected by the researchers between 9th February 2016 and 11th March 2016. Between these dates, individual interviews were conducted with 408 voluntary parents and the questionnaires were filled out.

Within the scope of the research, qualitative data was obtained through the interviews. Through semi-structured questions, the data collection process was completed between 1st March 2016 and 11th March 2016. Home visits were done for the interviews. As it was not allowed, voice recording was not performed in the interviews and the answers were recorded. Through the interview questions, data was collected from 20 parents and 20 children.

Collection of data obtained within the workshop was performed on 15th April 2016, the same date as the workshop. Within the workshop, the participants were divided into three groups and answers for the questions during the workshop question form were sought in line with a SWOT analysis study. Each group reported their answers in itself. Besides, opinions in regard to SWOT analysis were also shared and reported (Appendix-5).

The information obtained in this study, compiled the opinions workshop results and action plans have been established (Appendix-6).

2.6. Analysis of Data

Within the scope of the research, 408 items of data were collected from the Questionnaire on Mapping the Child Poverty in Mamak, 20 items of data through "Family Individual Interview Form" and 20 items of data through "Child Individual Interview Form".

General parent information obtained from the Questionnaire on Mapping the Child Poverty in Mamak, the information on the homes and the information on the children were analyzed using the SPSS 16.0 package program. In the data analysis, socio-demographic characteristics of the children and families were described using the information about frequency and percentage.

In order to analyze the data obtained with the qualitative interview form, the MAXQDA program was used. In the analysis of qualitative data, separate categories were developed for the answers given by the mothers and the children and as a result of these categories, the values were presented with suitable graphics. Concept maps are created as a result of the analysis of qualitative data (Appendix-7).

The analysis of the data obtained under the workshop has been formed as the workshop report. First of all groups evaluated in the report question the scope of the workshop and the workshop report in this direction has been established.

3. Findings

In this chapter, qualitative and quantative findings of research is presented under four headings: information of parents, information of children, in-depth interviews with parents and in-depth interviews with children.

In this chapter the research findings will be placed according to the quantitative research that is obtained through questionnaires and qualitative research obtained through interviews. The workshop was conducted within the scope of research to support quantitative and qualitative research data.

Findings of the first part of the conditions of life and demographic characteristics of parents who were included in the research findings are presented in Tables 3.1–3.55.

Findings of the second part of the demographic characteristics of children's of parents and parents' views of their children's child poverty are presented in Tables 3.26 to 3.58.

Findings on the in-depth interviews carried out in the third and fourth sections of the findings with parents and children are explained with graphics and the results are presented in Figures 3.1–3.22.

3.1. Findings Related to Parents

This section examines the distribution of the responses to the questions asked to determine the demographic characteristics and living conditions of the parents and results are given in the table in the form of frequency and percentage.

The findings of responses to questions according to parental types are presented in Table 3.1.

Table 3.1. Distributions According to Parents Who Answered the Survey

Respondent Parent	n	%
Mother	337	82,6
Father	69	16,9
Nonresponse	2	0,5
Total	408	100,0

As seen in Table 3.1 survey respondents are, 337 (82.6%) mother, 69 (16.9%) father. Two (0.5%) of the parents did not respond to this question. The status of respondent mothers' and fathers' ages are located in Table 3.2 and Table 3.3.

Table 3.2. Distributions According to Mothers' Ages

Respondent Mother's Age	n	%
Under 25	20	5,9
26–36	119	35,1
37–47	165	48,6
48–58	30	8,7
59 and above	4	1,1
Nonresponse	2	0,6
Total	339	100

As seen in Table 3.2. age of survey responded mothers are 165 (48,6%) of them are 37–47 years old, 119 (35,1%) of them are 26–36 years old, 30 (8,7%) of them are 48–58 years old, 20 (5,9%) of them are 15–25 years old, four (1,1%) of them are 59 years and above.

Table 3.3. Distributions According to Fathers' Ages

Respondent father's age	n	%
Under 25	1	1,5
26–36	19	27,5
37–47	30	43,5
48–58	17	24,6
59 and above	2	2,9
Total	69	100,0

Table 3.3 shows the age of fathers who responded to survey are 30 (43.5%) of them are 37–47 years old, 19 (27.5%) of them are 26–36 years old, 17 (24.6%) of them are 48–58 years old, two (2.9%) of them are 59 years old and older, and one (1.5%) of them is between 15–25 years old.

The status of spouse's ages of respondent mothers and fathers are located in Table 3.4 and 3.5.

Table 3.4. Distribution of Mothers' Spouses' Ages

Ages of respondent mother's spouses	n	%
15–25	8	2,3
26–36	75	22,1
37–47	147	43,5
48–58	59	17,4
59 and above	2	0,6
Nonresponse	48	14,1
Total	339	100

As seen in Table 3.4 spouses' ages of respondent mothers are 147 (43,5%) of the spouses are ages 37–47 years old, 75 (22,1%) of the spouse are ages 26–36 years old, 59 (17.4%) of the spouses are ages 48–58 years old, eight (2,3%) of the spouses are ages 15–25 years. 48 (14,1%) did not answer the question.

Table 3.5. Distribution of Fathers' Spouses' Ages

Ages of respondent father's spouses	n	%
15–25	6	8,7
26–36	21	30,4
37–47	30	43,5
48–58	11	16,0
59 and above	1	1,4
Total	69	100

As seen in Table 3.5 spouses' ages of survey respondent fathers are 30 (43.5%) of the spouses are ages 37–47, 21 (30.4%) of the spouses are ages 26–36, 11 (16.0%) of the spouses are 48–58 years old, six (8.7%) of the spouses are aged between 15–25 years old.

Distribution about the education status of respondent mothers and fathers and their spouses are located in Table 3.6 and 3.7.

Table 3.6. *Distributions of Mothers' and Their Spouses' Education Level*

Educational status of survey respondent mother's	n	%	Educational status of survey respondent father's spouse	n	%
Illiterate	40	11,8	Illiterate	24	7,1
Literate	47	13,9	Literate	23	6,8
Primary education	216	63,7	Primary education	211	62,2
High school dropout	7	2,0	High school dropout	9	2,7
High school	16	4,7	High school	21	6,2
Associate degree	2	0,6	Associate degree	0	0
University graduate	1	0,3	University graduate	3	0,9
Nonresponse	10	3,0	Nonresponse	48	14,1
Total	339	100	Total	339	100

As seen in Table 3.6. the respondent mothers; 216 (63.7%) of them are primary school graduates, 47 (13.9%) of them illiterate, 40 (11.8%) of them literate, 16 (4.7%) of them high school graduates, seven (2.0%) of them high school dropout, two (0.6%) of them have an associate degree, one (0.3%) has a university degree level of education. Ten (3.0%) mothers did not answer the question. Investigating the respondent mothers spouse's educational status, 211 (62.2%) of them primary school graduates, 24 (7.1%) of them illiterate, 23 (6.8%) of them literate, 21 (6% 2) of them high school, nine (2.7%) of them high school drop out, three (0.9%) of them seen as having a university degree level of education. 48 (14.1%) of mothers did not answer the question.

Table 3.7. *Distributions of Fathers' and Their Spouses' Education Level*

Educational status of survey respondent father's	n	%	Educational status of survey respondent father's spouses	n	%
Illiterate	4	5,8	Illiterate	13	18,9
Literate	4	5,8	Literate	8	11,6
Primary education	47	68,1	Primary education	38	55,1
High school dropout	6	8,7	High school dropout	4	5,6
High school	5	7,2	High school	3	4,4
Associate degree	1	1,5	Associate degree	0	0
University graduate	0	0	University graduate	0	0
Nonresponse	2	2,9	Nonresponse	3	4,4
Total	69	100	Total	69	100

As seen in Table 3.7. respondent fathers graduation levels are 47 (68.1%) of them primary school, six (8.7%) of them high school drop out, five (7.2%) of them high school, four (5.8%) of them illiterate, four (5.8%) of them literate, one (1.5%) of them have an associate degree level of education. From the response of the survey respondent fathers about the spouse's educational status 38 (55.1%) of them primary school, 13 (18.9%) of them illiterate, eight (11.6%) of them literate, four (5,6%) of them high school drop out, three (4.4%) of them appear to be a high school graduate. Two (2.9%) fathers did not answer the question about their educational status, and three (4.4%) of them for their spouse's educational status.

Distribution of marriage status of the parents who responded to the survey are located in Table 3.8.

Table 3.8. Distributions According to Parents' Marital Status

	Marital status of the respondent father		Marital status of the respondent mother	
	n	%	n	%
Marital Status				
Officially Married	63	91,3	241	71,9
Common-law Marriage	0	0	7	2,1
Divorced	5	7,2	69	20,6
Widow (Death of partner)	1	1,5	18	5,4
Total	69	100	335	100
Number of Marriage				
1. marriage	18	26,1	106	31,6
2. marriage	4	5,8	13	3,9
3. marriage	0	0	1	0,3
4. marriage	0	0	2	0,6
Nonresponse	47	68,1	213	63,6
Total	69	100	335	100
Year of Marriage				
1–5	4	5,8	17	5,1
6–10	14	20,3	42	12,5
11–15	21	30,5	62	18,5
16–20	14	20,3	73	21,8
21 and above	10	14,4	59	17,6
Nonresponse	6	8,7	82	24,5
Total	69	100	335	100

	Marital status of the respondent father		Marital status of the respondent mother	
	n	%	n	%
Marriage Age				
13–17	7	10,1	132	39,4
18–22	27	39,1	125	37,3
23–27	22	31,9	37	11,0
28–32	7	10,1	10	2,9
33 and above	2	2,9	2	0,6
Nonresponse	4	5,8	29	8,6
Total	69	100	335	100

As seen in Table 3.8. fathers who participated in the survey 63 (91.3%) are officially married, there is no father who has a common-law marriage. While divorced fathers are five (7.2%), one (1.5%) is widowed. When looked at the situation of mothers participating in the study, 241 (71.9%) of them are officially married, 69 (20.6%) of these are divorced, 18 (5.4%) widowed, seven (2.1%) of them are common-law married.

When married father's marriage number is examined 18 (26.1%) are in their first marriage, four of them (5.8%) seems to have a second marriage, and 47 (68.1%) of fathers did not answer the question. When the married mother's marriage number is examined 106 (31.6%) are in first marriage, 13 (3.9%) have a second marriage, two (0.6%) of them are in their fourth marriage, one (0.3%) one is in their third marriage. 213 (63.6%) mothers did not answer this question.

When looked at the status in terms of the marriage years of fathers surveyed, 21 (30.5%) of them are between 11–15 years, 14 (20.3%) of them between 6–10 years, 14 (20.3%) of them between 16–20 years, 10 (14.4%) of them more than 21 years, four (5.8%) of them married between 1–5 years. Six (8.7%), fathers did not answer the question. When data examined relating to the marriage years of mothers who responded to the survey, 73 (21.8%) between 16–20 years, 62 (18.5%) between 11–15 years, 59 (17.6%) more than 21 years, 42 (12.5%) between 6–10 years, 17 (5.1%) are married between 1–5 years. 82 (24.5%) mothers did not answer this question. When the data is examined related to the marriage age of fathers 27 (39.1%) were aged 18–22, 22 (31.9%) were aged 23–27, seven (10.1%) were aged 13–17, seven (10.1%) were aged 28–32, two (2.9%) of them

40

were 33 years old when they married. Four (5.8%), of the fathers did not answer the question. When the marriage age of mothers were examined 132 (39.4%) were 13–17 years of age, 125 (37.3%) were 18–22 years of age, 37 (11.0%) were 23–27 years of age, 10 (2,9%) of them were 28–32 years of age, two (0.6%) of them are observed to be married older than the age of 33.

Distributions according to divorce reasons and alimony status of parents are located in Table 3.9.

Table 3.9. Distributions According to Divorce Reasons and Alimony Status of Parents

Reason for Divorce	n	%
Financial problems	24	19,2
Unemployment	12	9,6
Violence	38	30,4
Habits such as alcohol-gambling	21	16,8
Relationship with someone else	10	8
Other	12	9,6
Nonresponse	8	6,4
Total	125	100
Alimony Status		
Yes	7	9,5
No	67	90,5
Total	74	100,0
Amount of Alimony		
0–200 TL	1	14,3
201–400 TL	4	57,1
401–600 TL	2	28,6
Total	7	100

As shown in Table 3.9. parents of 38 (30.4%) have violence, 24 (19.2%) have financial difficulties, 21 (16.8%) have habits such as alcohol-gambling, 12 (9,6%) of them are unemployed, 10 (8%) of them were separated because of the relationship with someone else. 12 (9.6%) of respondents were separated from their spouses for other reasons. Those who divorced from their spouses for other reasons, three (2.4%) of them due to disagreement, three (2.4%) were due to conflict, two (1.6%) of them for having disabled children, one (0.8%) due to going abroad, one (0.8%) from drug addiction, one (0.8%) for having problems with children, one (0.8%) reported that they divorced due to psychological violence.

67 (90.5%) divorced people do not receive alimony from the spouses, seven (9.5%) of them receive alimony. When considering the amount of the alimony received four (57,1%) receive 201–400 TL (Turkish Liras); two (28.6%) receive 401–600 TL; one (14.3%) gets 0–200 TL.

Distributions of parents' status according to received monthly payment from widow/orphan/ parental are included in Table 3.10.

Table 3.10. Distributions of Parents' Status According to Received Monthly Payment from Widow/Orphan/ Parental

Monthly Payment Status Received From Parents	n	%
Yes	5	5,2
No	88	91,7
Nonresponse	3	3,1
Total	96	100,0
Amount of Monthly Payment Received From Parents		
201–400 TL	1	12,5
401–600 TL	2	25
601 TL and above	2	25
Nonresponse	3	37,5
Total	8	100,0
Status for Receiving Widows and Orphans Payment		
Yes	8	42,1
No	11	57,9
Nonresponse	0	
Total	19	100,0
Amount of Widows and Orphans Payment		
401–600 TL	4	50
601 TL and above	4	50
Total	8	100,0

As seen in Table 3.10, 88 (91.7%) of the parents are not receiving payment from their mother and father, there are five (5.2%) people getting monthly payment from their parents. There are three (3.1%) parents who did not respond to this question. When looked in terms of monthly amounts received from parents, two (25%) people receives 601 TL and above; two (25%) people receives 401–600 TL; one (12.5%) person receives 201–400 TL.

When the status is examined for the widows and orphans monthly payment received from the state, 11 (57.9%) people are not receiving aid, eight (42.1%) people are receiving aid. In terms of monthly amount received, four (50%) parents receives 601 TL and over; four (50%) parents receives 401–600 TL.

Distribution about birth and migration status of the parent's located in Table 3.11.

Table 3.11. Distributions of Parents' Migration and Birth Informations

	Survey Respondent Father's		Survey Respondent Mother's	
Place of Birth	n	%	n	%
Province	35	50,7	237	69,9
District	23	33,3	67	19,8
Town / Village	11	16,0	31	9,1
Nonresponse	0	0	4	1,2
Total	69	100	339	100
Migration Status				
Yes	29	42,0	106	31,3
No	38	55,1	218	64,3
Nonresponse	2	2,9	15	4,4
Total	69	100	339	100
Place of Migration				
Town / Village	11	34,4	23	22,4
District	8	25	37	36,0
Province	8	25	40	38,8
Abroad	1	3,1	2	1,9
Nonresponse	4	12,5	1	0,9
Total	32	100	103	100
Time of Migration				
0–2 Years	3	10,7	9	8,4
3–5 Years	9	32,1	3	2,9

	Survey Respondent Father's		Survey Respondent Mother's	
Time of Migration	n	%	n	%
6–11 Years	5	17,9	32	29,9
12–20 Years	4	14,3	36	33,6
21 years and above	6	21,4	26	24,3
Nonresponse	1	3,6	1	0,9
Total	28	100	107	100
Reason for Migration				
Job opportunities	17	67,4	53	22,3
Children's education	2	7,7	5	2,1
Marriage	2	7,7	43	18,2
Health problems	3	11,4	126	53,2
Security	0	0	1	0,4
Other	1	3,9	7	3,0
Nonresponse	1	3,9	2	0,8
Total	26	100	237	100
Number of Years Lived in Ankara				
0–2 Years	4	5,8	7	2,1
3–5 Years	7	10,1	7	2,1
6–11 Years	6	8,9	39	11,5
12–20 Years	14	20,3	59	17,4
21 Years and above	35	50,6	207	61,0
Nonresponse	3	4,3	20	5,9
Total	69	100	339	100

As seen in Table 3.11. 35 (50,7%) fathers born in the province, 23 (33,3) were in the district, 11 (16.0%) of them born in town/village. When the status of mothers are examined, 237 (69.9%) of them in the province, 67 (19.8%) in district, 31 (9.1%) of them was born in town/village.

38 (55.1%) of fathers stated that they did not emigrate, 29 (42.0%) stated that they emigrated. Two (2.9%) fathers did not respond the survey. 218 (64,3%) mothers said that they did not emigrate, 106 (31.3%) of them stated that they emigrated. 15 (4.4%) mothers did not answer the question. When the father's place of migration is asked 11 (34.4%) of them from village/town, eight (25%) from districts, eight (25%) of them from province,

one (3.1%) stated he had migrated from abroad. Four (12.5%) fathers did not answer this question. When the mothers' response on the place of migration is examined, 40 (38.8%) of them from province, 37 (36.0%) from district, 23 (22.4%) from village/town, two (1.9%) of them stated that they migrated from abroad.

Survey participant mothers and fathers were asked about time of immigration. Nine (32.1%) of fathers was 3–5 years ago, six (21.4%) of them more than 21 years ago, five (17.9%) 6–11 years ago, four (14% 3) 12–20 years ago, three (10.7%) of them stated that they emigrated 0–2 years ago. One (3.6%) father did not answer the question. When the responses of mothers are examined 36 (33.6%) of them from 12–20 years ago, 32 (29.9%) 6–11 years ago, 26 (24.3%) of them 21 years ago, nine (8, 4%) of them 0–2 years ago, three (2.9%) stated that they emigrated 3–5 years ago.

Mothers and fathers were asked about the reason for migration. 17 (67.4%) of fathers due to job opportunities, three (11.4%) due to health problems, two (7.7%) for their children's education, two (7.7%) of them stated that they migrated due to marriage. One father (3.6%) stated that he emigrated due to terrorism. When the responses of mothers are examined 126 (53.2%) due to health problems, 53 (22.3%) for job opportunities, 43 (18.2%) due to marriage, five (2.1%) for their children's education, one (0.4%) stated that they migrated for security reasons. Seven (3%) mothers gave the other response. Responses for other include two (0,8%) of terror, two (0.8%) have urban transformation, one (0.4%) foreign citizenship revocation, one (0.4%) for family reasons, one (0.4%) has the answer such as obligation.

Mothers and fathers who participated to the survey were asked about the number of years they have been living in Ankara. 35 (50,6%) of fathers more than 21 years, 14 (20.3%) of them 12–20 years, seven (10.1%) of them are 3–5 years, six (8.9%) are 6–11 years, four (5.8%) lives in Ankara 0–2 years. 207 (61.0%) mothers are longer than 21 years, 59 (17.4%) of them 12–20 years, 39 (11.5%) of them 6–11 years, seven (2.1%) of them 3–5 years, seven (2.1%) of them are living in Ankara for 0–2 years.

In Table 3.12. distribution of the parents' debt who responded to the survey are located.

Table 3.12. Distributions of Parents' Debt Status

Debt Status	n	%
Yes	357	87,5
No	47	11,5
Nonresponse	4	1,0
Total	408	100,0
Debt Amount		
0–500 TL	18	5,0
501–1500 TL	40	11,0
1501–3000 TL	67	18,5
3001–5000 TL	57	15,8
5001 TL and above	174	48,3
Nonresponse	5	1,4
Total	361	100
Borrows to		
Person	90	18,75
Tradesmen (grocery etc.)	41	8,5
Landlord	18	3,75
Store	42	8,75
Bank	226	55,4
Bill debt	44	9,2
Other	7	1,5
Nonresponse	12	2,5
Total	480	100

As seen in Table 3.12., 357 (87.7%) parents are in debt; 47 (11.5%) do not have any debt. Three (0.7%) parents did not answer this question. In terms of the amount of debt that parents owed; 174 (42.6%) parents owe 5001 lira and above, 67 (16.4%) of them owe between 1501–3000 TL, 57 (14%) of them owe between 3001–5000 TL, 40 (9.8%) of them owe between 501–1500 TL and 18 (4.4%) owe between 0–500 TL.

When looked from the perspective of the place owed to 226 (55.4%) parents to the bank, 90 (18,75%) of them to a person, 44 (9.2%) due to the bill debt to the government, 42 (8.75%) of them to stores, 41 (8.5%) of them to trader's (grocery, etc.), 18 (3.75%) of them to the landlord, seven (1.5%) parents reported that they have other debts. One out of the seven people indicated that have other debt has vehicle liability who do not have any vehicle.

The distribution of the parents' health insurance status is given in Table 3.13.

Table 3.13. The Distributions of the Parents' Health Insurance Status

Health Insurance	n	%
N.A	34	8,3
SSK	90	22,1
BAĞKUR	11	2,7
Retirement Box	7	1,7
Green Card	260	63,7
Nonresponse	6	1,5
Total	408	100,0

As seen in Table 4.13., it was determined that 260 (63,7%) of parents are green card holders, 11 (2,7%) parents have BAGKUR, seven (1,7%) parents have retirement box for their health insurance. 34 (8,3%) parents do not have health insurance.

The distribution of income and employment status of the parents are presented in Table 3.14.

Table 3.14. The Distributions of the Parents' Income and Employment Status

Employment Status	n	%
Yes	68	16,7
Retired	12	2,9
No	319	78,2
Nonresponse	9	2,2
Total	408	100
Work Type		
Construction worker	6	8,8
Peddler	2	2,9
Industrial worker	10	14,8
Casual workers	31	45,6
Babysitter / hand worker	4	5,9
Other	15	22,1
Total	68	100,0

Spouse's Employment Status	n	%
Yes	138	33,8
No	147	36
Nonresponse	123	30,1
Total	408	100,0
Other People Working in the Family		
Yes	21	5,1
No	158	38,7
Nonresponse	229	56,1
Total	408	100,0
Average Income of the Family		
0 TL	149	36,5
0–400 TL	105	25,7
401–800 TL	65	15,9
801–1200 TL	62	15,2
1201–1600 TL	18	4,4
1601–2000	9	2,2
2001 and above TL	408	100

When Table 3.14 was examined, it was determined that 319 (78,2%) parents do not work, only 68 (16,7%) parents have a job, 12 (2,9%) parents are retired. When working parents aare analyzed about terms of their jobs, it was determined that 31 (46,5%) parents are casual workers, 10 (14,8%) parents are industrial workers, six (8,8%) parents are construction workers, four (5,9%) parents are babysitters and hand workers, two (2,9%) parents are peddlers and 15 (22,1%) parents work in other jobs. It was respected that other parents who answered the question 'other', work as paper and plastic collectors, cleaners, furniture manufacturers, doormen, hairdressers, security and service officers.

When the parents' spouses' employment status were examined, it was determined that 147 (36%) of spouses do not have a job, 138 (33,8%) of spouses have a job. When the results of question 'Are there other people working in the family?' was examined, it was determined that 21 (5,1%) of them have another working person in their family.

When the average income in the family was invastigated, parents stated that 149 (36,5%) parents have 400 Turkish Lira and under average income,

105 (25,7%) of them have 401–800 Lira, 65 (15,9%) of them have 801–1200 Lira, 62 (15,2%) of them have 1201–1600 Lira, 44 (10,8%) of them 0 Lira, 18 (4,4%) of them have 1601 Lira and above; and nine (2,2%) of them did not give an answer to this question.

Distribution of the periods that parents do not have a job are given in Table 3.15.

Table 3.15. Distribution of the Periods That Parents Do Not Have a Job

Unemployed Status for Both Spouses	n	%
Yes	266	65,2
No	19	4,7
Never worked	68	16,7
Nonresponse	55	13,5
Total	408	100,0
Number of Years Worked		
0–6 month	15	4,6
7 month–1 year	13	4,02
1–2 year	9	2,8
2–3 year	130	40,2
3 year and above	138	42,7
None	18	5,6
Total	323	100,0
Economic Status During Spouse's Unemployment		
Relative's help	91	16,1
Neighbor's help	42	7,4
Municipality	214	38
Foundation	39	7
Welfare	138	24,5
Other	10	1,8
Nonresponse	30	5,3
Total	564	100

When the results of the status of spouses' unemployment were examined at Table 3.15, it was determined that 266 (65,2%) of parents' spouses were unemployed, 68 (16,7%) spouses never worked; 19 (4,7%) spouses were never unemployed. 138 (42,7%) parents determined that they have been unemployed for the last three years and above, 130 (40,2%) parents two to three years, 18 (5,6%) parents determined that they never worked. 15 (4,6%) parents who are unemployed did not have a job for six months and above, 13 (4,02%) parents who are unemployed did not have a job for seven months to one year. When the results of how the parents ensure their livelihood when one spouse is unemployed were analyzed, 214 (38%) of them answered the question they get help from municipality, 138 (24,5%) get help from social assistance and solidarity foundation, 91 (16,1%) of them from their relatives, 42 (7,5%) of them from their neighbors, 39 (7%) of them from foundations, 10 (1,8%) of them answered they get help from other help systems, 30 (5,3%) parents did not answer this question. It was determined that parents who answered the question 'other' provide their livelihood with old savings, widow's pension, bank interest, unemployment benefits, help from a former spouse, cleaning, religious assistance, staying at the house of their friends, getting children allowance, getting help from neighbors, borrowing and getting help from state.

Distribution of the parents' situations of willingness to work are given in Table 3.16.

Table 3.16. Distribution of the Parents' Situations of Willingness to Work

Willingness to Work with Regular Income	n	%
Yes	279	68,4
No	76	18,7
Nonresponse	53	13
Total	408	100,0
Reason for Willingness to Work		
To get what I want	62	17,9
To support my spouse	79	22,7
To meet the needs of my children	146	42
To pay our debts	54	15,6
Other	3	0,9
Nonresponse	3	0,9
Total	347	100
Reason for Refusing to Work		
My spouse does not allow	18	21,7
Because of my health problems	20	24,1
There is nobody to look after my children	40	48,2

Reason for Refusing to Work	n	%
I can't find work	3	3,6
Due to old age	2	2,8
Total	83	100
Earned money spent on		
Kitchen expenses	85	22,5
Heating	16	4,2
Debts	101	26,8
Children's education	32	8,5
Other	4	1
Nonresponse	140	37
Total	378	100

As seen in Table 3.16, it was determined that 279 (68,4%) of parents want to work with ra egular income, 76 (18,7%) of parents do not want to work with a regular income. When the reasons of wanting to work were examined, 146 (42%) parents want to meet the needs of thei children, 79 (22,7%) to support their spouses, 62 (17,9%) to get what their children want, 54 (15,6%) to pay their debts, three (0,9%) want for other reasons. Parents who answered the question 'other' stated that want to have a regular job to stand on their own two feet, to retire and to live in a better place.

When the reasons of refusing to work were examined, it was seen that 40 (48,2%) parents stated that there is nobody to look after their children, 20 (24,1%) because of their health problems, 18 (21,7%) of their spouses do not allow, three (3,2%) stated that other reasons like cannot find a job, due to old age, they tried but they cannot. According to the table it is stated that earned money is spent on debt for 101 (26,8%), kitchen costs for 85 (22,5%), children's education for 32 (8,5%), heating costs for 16 (4,2%).

Distribution of the parents' health situations are given in Table 3.17.

Table 3.17. Distribution of the Parents' Health Situations

Situations of Health Problems in Household	n	%
Yes	119	29,2
No	286	70,1
Nonresponse	3	0,7
Total	408	100,0
Person on Medication		
Yes	92	22,5
No	310	76,0
Nonresponse	6	1,5
Total	408	100,0
Situations of Medication Given by the State		
Yes	74	80,5
No	18	19,6
Total	92	100,0
Disabled Person in Family		
Yes	67	16,4
No	333	81,6
Nonresponse	8	2,0
Total	408	100,0
Disabled Person Support by the State		
2022	32	45,1
Home care support money	17	24
No	22	31
Total	71	100,0
Support Allowance for Disabled Person		
0–200 TL	5	10,2
201–400 TL	16	32,7
401–600 TL	7	14,3
601–800 TL	7	14,3
801 and above	14	28,6
Total	49	100,0
Type of Aid		
Shelter	206	17,3
Food	327	27,5
Clothing	64	5,4
Education	186	15,7

Type of Aid	n	%
Health	258	21,7
Disability allowance	36	3
None of them	18	1,5
Other	92	7,7
Nonresponse	4	0,3
Total	1191	100
Status of Receiving Health Care Aid		
Yes	357	87,5
No	43	10,5
Nonresponse	8	2,0
Total	408	100,0
Reason for not receiving health care aid		
We do not have health insurance	30	70
We do not have time	1	2,3
Other	8	18,6
Nonresponse	4	9,3
Total	43	100,0

According to the Table 3.17, it was determined that 286 (70,1%) parents do not have a health problem in their family, 119 (29,2%) parents have a health problem in their family, 92 (22,5%) families have a person who gets medication. It was seen that 74 (80,5%) of health people's medication is covered by the state, 18 (19,6%) of health people's medication is not covered by the state.

It was determined that 67 (16,4%) parents included in the study have a disabled person in their family, 32 (45,1%) of them get aid according to Law No. 2022, 17 (24%) of them get home care support money, 16 (32,7%) of disabled people get 201–400 Lira, 14 (28,6%) get 801 Lira and above, seven (14,3%) get 401–600 Lira, 14 (28,6%) of them get 601–800 Lira, five (10,2%) of them get 200 Lira and under aid from state.

357 (87,5%) families who participated in the study get health care aid, 43 (10,5%) of them do not get health care aid. When causes of cannot receive health care aid were examined, it was determine that 30 (70%) of them do not have health insurance, eight (18,6%) of them listed other reasons. Some parents who answered this question as 'other' stated that

they are retired from social security institution and some of them stated that they do not know why they do not have health care aid.

According to the table, parents stated that 327 (27,5%) of them get food aid, 258 (21,7%) health care aid, 206 (17,3%) shelter aid, 186 (%15,7) education aid, 64 (5,4%) clothing aid, 36 (3%) aid for disabled person, 92 (57,7%) get other types of aid and 18 (1,5%) do not get any aid. Parents who answered the question as 'other' stated that 84 (7%) get coal aid, 38 (0,25%) children allowance, one (0,08%) rent help, one (0,08%) gets bread aid.

Distribution of the mental condition of the parents are given in Table 3.18.

Table 3.18. *Distribution of the Mental Condition of the Parents*

Duration of Being Extremely Unhappy/ Feeling In Depression During The Last Week	n	%
Never felt depressed	73	17,9
1–2	82	20,1
3–4	74	18,1
5–7	175	42,9
Nonresponse	4	1,0
Total	408	100,0
Loss of Interest Long-Term		
Yes	272	66,6
No	132	32,4
Nonresponse	4	1,0
Total	408	100,0
Feeling in Depression for two years		
Yes	299	73,2
No	105	25,7
Nonresponse	4	1
Total	408	100,0

As seen in Table 3.18, 175 (42,9%) felt depressed 5–7 times, 82 (20,9%) 1–2 times, 74 (18,1%) felt depressed 3–4 times for last week; 73 (17,9%) of them did not feel depressed.

272 (66,6%) of parents stated that they feel a loss of interests for long term, and 132 (32,4%) of them stated that they do not feel loss of interests for long term. 299 (73,2%) of parents felt depressed for two years and 105 of parents stated that they did not feel depressed for two years.

The distribution of parents' shopping places and food consumptions frequency are given in Table 3.19.

Table 3.19. Distribution of Parents' Shopping Places and Food Consumption Frequency

Place for Kitchen Shopping	n	%
Bazaar	308	52,9
Market	189	32,5
Peddler	38	6,5
Fruitseller	3	0,5
Grocery	22	3,8
Other	17	2,9
Nonresponse	5	0,8
Total	582	100
Shopping for Clothing		
Store	132	24,2
Bazaar	178	32,6
Peddler	47	8,6
Second Hand	33	6
Relative/Neighbor	71	13
From Aids	85	15,6
Total	546	100
Frequency of Meat Consumption		
Several times a week	2	0,5
Once a week	24	5,9
Once a month	143	35
Several times a year	68	16
None	169	41,4
Nonresponse	2	0,5
Total	408	100,0
Frequency of Dairy Products Consumption		
Almost every day	32	7,8
Several times a week	133	32,6
Once a week	126	30,9
Once a year	108	26,5
None	6	1,5
Nonresponse	3	0,7
Total	408	100,0

Frequency of Vegetable Consumption	n	%
Almost every day	6	1,5
Several times a week	70	17,2
Once a week	159	39,0
Once a month	164	40,2
None	7	1,7
Nonresponse	2	0,5
Total	408	100,0
Frequency of Fruit Consumption		
Almost every day	3	0,7
Several times a week	26	6,4
Once a week	132	32,4
Once a month	224	55
Several times a year	17	4,2
None	4	1,0
Nonresponse	2	0,5
Total	408	100,0

As seen in the Table 3.19, it was determined that 308 (52,9%) parents shop from a bazaar for their kitchen needs, 189 (32,5%) parents from market, 38 (6,5%) parents from peddler, 22 (3,8%) parents from grocery, 17 (2,9%) parents from other ways, three (0,5%) of them shop from a fruitseller for their kitchen needs. three (0,5%) parents who shop for their kitchen needs from other ways stated that they collect rotten goods from market, four (0,7%) of them stated that they get help, one (0,1%) stated that he gets help from his neighbors.

When the results from the places that they do their clothes shopping were examined, it was seen that 178 (32,6%) shop from a bazaar, 132 (24,2%) from stores, 85 (15,6%) from aids, 71 (13%) from relatives/neighbors, 47 (8,6%) from a peddler, 33 (6%) of them shop for their clothes from second hand.

When frequency of meat consumption was examined parents stated that 169 (41,4%) parents never eat meat, 143 (35%) parents eat meat once a month, 68 (16%) of them several times a year, 24 (5,9%) of them once a week, two (0,5%) of them eat meat several times a week.

When frequency of dairy products consumption was examined it was determined that 133 (32,6%) of them several times a week, 126 (30,9%)

of them once a week, 108 (26,5%) of them once a month, 32 (7,8%) of them almost every day consume dairy products and six (1,5%) parents never consume dairy product.

When frequency of vegetable consumption was examined it was determined that 164 (40,2%) parents once a month, 159 (39%) once a week, 70 (17,2%) several times a week, six (1,5%) of them almost every day consume vegetables and seven (1,7%) parents never consume vegetables.

When frequency of fruit consumption was examined it was determined that 224 (55%) parents once a month, 132 (32,4%) of them once a week, 26 (6,4%) several times a week, 17 (4,2%) several times a year, three (0,7%) of them almost every day consume fruit and four (1%) parents never consume fruit.

The distribution of the type and status of houses which parents live in are presented in Table 3.20.

Table 3.20. Distribution of the Type and Status of Houses Which Parents Live

Type of House	n	%
Slum	57	14,0
Detached house	13	3,2
Flat	335	82,1
Nonresponse	3	0,7
Total	408	100,0
Status of House		
Rent	190	46,6
Homeowner	202	49,5
Belongs to parent	5	1,2
Belongs to mother/father-in-law	2	0,5
Belongs to benevolent person	3	0,7
Nonresponse	6	1,5
Total	408	100,0
Monthly Rent Amount		
0–200 TL	92	48,5
201–400 TL	67	35,2
401–600 TL	28	14,7
601–800 TL	1	0,5
Nonresponse	2	1,1
Total	190	100,0

Number of Rooms in the House	n	%
One	4	1,0
Two	272	66,7
Three	87	21,3
Four	35	8,6
Five and more	1	0,2
Nonresponse	9	2,2
Total	408	100,0
Inside Structure of House		
Separate kitchen	168	16,5
Kitchen is not separate	163	16
Bathroom is separate	82	8,1
Toilet and Bathroom is Separate	276	27,2
Toilet is inside the house	284	28
Toilet is outside the house	6	0,6
Nonresponse	36	3,5
Total	1015	100

Items That is not At Home	Have		Do not Have		Unanswered	
	n	%	n	%	n	%
Fridge	400	98	5	1,27	3	0,73
Television	397	97,30	8	1,97	3	0,73
Washing machine	289	70,83	116	28,44	3	0,73
Computer	43	10,53	362	88,74	3	0,73
Iron	212	51,96	193	47,31	3	0,73
Telephone	11	2,7	394	96,57	3	0,73
Oven	191	46,8	214	52,47	3	0,73
Dishwasher	71	17,40	334	81,87	3	0,73
Vacuum cleaner	252	61,76	153	37,51	3	0,73
Heater	200	49,01	205	50,26	3	0,73
Mobile phone	385	94,36	20	4,91	3	0,73
Tablet	10	2,45	395	96,82	3	0,73

When Table 3.20 was examined., it was determined that 335 (82.1%) parents live in a flat, 57 (14%) in slums, 13 (3.2%) in a detached house, 202(49,5%) in their own house, 190 (46,6%) in a rented house. Five (1.2%) parents live in their parent's house, three (0.7%) parents live in benevolent person's house, two (0.5%) of them live in mother in-law/father-in-law's house. 92 (22.7%) parents pay 0–200 TL for rent, 67 (16.5%) of them

201–400 TL, 28 (6.9%) of them 401–600 TL, one (0.2%) parent pays 601–800 TL for rent.

When the number of rooms in the parents' house were examined, it was determined that 272 (66.7%) have two rooms, 87 (21.3%) have three rooms, 35 (8.6%) have four rooms, four (1%) have one room, one (0.2%) has five or more rooms, and 284 (28%) parents have the toilet inside the house, 276 (27.2%) have bathroom and toilet together, 168 (16.5%) have the separate kitchen, 163 (16%) do not have separate kitchen, 82 (8.1%) have separate bathrooms, six (0.6%) do not have toilet inside house.

When belongings parents have in their house were examined, it was determined that 400 (98%) parents have a fridge, 397 (97,30%) parents have a television, 289 (70,83%) parents have a washing machine, 43 (10,53%) parents have a computer, 212 (51,96%) parents have an iron, 11 (2,7%) parents have a telephone, 191 (46,8%) parents have an oven, 71 (17,40%) parents have a dishwasher, 252 (61,76%) parents have a vacuum cleaner, 200 (49,01%) have a heater, 385 (94,36%) parents have a mobile phone, and 10 (2,45%) parents have a tablet in their house.

Distribution of the number of people that parents live with and relationship status are presented in Table 3.21.

Table 3.21. Distribution of the Number of People That Parents Live with and Relationship Status

Number of People Residing at Home	n	%
1	3	0,7
2	34	8,3
3	80	19,6
4	149	36,5
5	86	21,1
6	36	8,8
7 and above	15	3,6
Nonresponded	5	1,0
Status of Relatives Residing At Home		
Yes	24	5,9
No	379	92,9
Nonresponse	5	1,2
Total	408	100,0

Relatives Residing At Home	n	%
Mother-Father	12	50
Mother-Father-in-law	9	37,5
Sister/Brother	1	4,2
Sister/Brother of my spouse	1	4,2
Other	1	4,2
Total	24	100

According to Table 3.21., it was determined that 149 (36,5) of parents live in a four person family, 86 (21,1%) live in a five person family, 80 (19,6%) live in a three person family, 36 (8,8%) parents live in a six person family, 34 (8,3%) live in a three person family, 15 (3,6%) people live a seven person and above family, three (0,7%) parents live alone.

Parents stated that 379 (92,9%) of them do not reside with a relative, 24 (5,9%) of them reside with a relative at home. 12 (50%) parents who reside with a relative stated that they live with their mothers and fathers, nine (37,5%) live with mother-in-law/father-in-law, one (4,2%) lives with their sister/brother, one (4,1%) parent lives with their spouse's sister/brother.

"What kind of energy do you provide your heating needs with?", "What are you warming up with?", "How do you meet your water needs?" and "What do you cook your food with" questions related with houses' heating and fuel were asked to parents. The responses received from parents are given in Table 3.22.

Table 3.22. Distributions of Parents' Heating, Cooking and Reaching Drink Water Status

Heating Types	n	%
Natural gas	109	26,7
Electricity	5	1,2
Wood	5	1,2
Coal	248	60,8
Wood and Coal	34	8,3
Other	1	0,2
Nonresponse	6	1,5
Total	408	100,0

Heating Tool	n	%
Stove	66	16,2
Joint or central heating radiators	245	60,0
The boiler heating system	86	21,1
Other	3	0,7
Nonresponse	8	2,0
Total	408	100,0
Cooking Meal		
Bottled gas	288	67,6
Natural gas	96	22,5
Electricity	1	0,2
Wood	12	2,8
Coal	23	5,4
Unanswered	6	1,4
Total	426	100
Drink Water		
Tap water from home	390	95,6
Away from tap water	12	2,9
Carboy/ready water	1	0,2
Nonresponse	5	1,2
Total	408	100,0

When Table 3.22. was examined, it was determined that 248 (60,9%) parents use coal for heating, 109 (26.7%) use natural gas, 34 (8.3%) use both wood and coal, five (1,2%) use electricity, five (1.2%) use wood for heating, and most of them (60%) have central heating systems at their houses.

When the results about cooking a meal were examined, 288 (67,6%) parents use bottled gas, 96 (22.5%) natural gas, 23 (5.4%) coal, 12 (2,8%) wood and one (0.2%) uses electricity to cook their meal.

When the results about reaching drinking water were examined, it was determined that 390 (95,6%) of parents use tap water from their home, 12 (2,9%) tap water outside, one (0,02%) uses carboy/ready water.

The distributions of parents' complaints about their houses are given in Table 3.23.

Table 3.23. Distributions of Parents' Complaints About Their Houses

Complaints About House	n	%
Inadequate number of rooms	241	32,7
Very cold	238	32,3
The dampness of the house	85	11,5
Lack of Bathroom/Toilet	4	0,5
Security issue	115	15,6
Insects/Mice	14	1,9
Not enough lighting	8	1
Others (Infrastructure, sound system, manual labor, etc.)	10	1,4
Nonresponse	22	3
Total	737	100

When table 3.23 was examined, 241 (32.7%) parents complain about the number of rooms being inadequate, 238 (32.3%) cold homes, 115 (15.6%) security issue, 85 (11.5%) damp house, 14 (1.9%) insects and mice, eight (1%) not enough lighting, and four (0.5%) lack of bathroom and toilets. One (0,01%) answered the question 'other' complains about infrastructure, one (0,01%) sound system, one (0,01%) manual labor, one (0,01%) of them complains about having a house far from city centre.

The distribution of the numbers of changing home of parents are presented in Table 3.24.

Table 3.24. Distribution of the Numbers of Changing Home

Number of Changing Home for Last Two Years	n	%
Never	240	58,8
1	112	27,5
2	31	7,6
3 and above	15	3,6
Nonresponse	10	2,5
Total	408	100,0

As seen in the Table 3.24, 240 (58,8%) of parents never changed their home for two years, 112 (27,5%) of parents once, 31 (7,6%) of parents two times, 15 (3,6%) of them changed their homes three times and above for last two years.

Distribution of the status related to parents of children left alone at home without adult supervision findings were given in Table 3.25.

Table 3.25. Distribution of the Status Related to Parents of Children Left Alone at Home Without Adult Supervision

Children Left Alone at Home Without Adult Supervision	n	%
Yes	14	3,4
No	389	95,3
Nonresponse	5	1,3
Total	408	100,0

As seen in Table 3.25., the majority of parents (95.3%) do not leave their children alone at home.

3.2. Findings Belonging to Children

In the context of research parents has been asked information about their children. The demographic characteristics of children of parents and parents views of their children's child poverty are presented in Tables 3.26 to 3.55.

The distribution of the number of children that parents have are given in Table 3.26.

Table 3.26. Distributions Related to Number of Children Parents Have

Number of Children	n	%
One	72	17,6
Two	154	37,7
Three	113	27,7
Four	49	12,0
Five and Above	16	4,0
Nonresponse	4	1,0
Total	408	100,0

When Table 3.26., is examined it is determined that 154 (37.7%) parents have two children, 113 (27.7%) parents have three, 72 (17.6%) have one, 49 (12%) have four, 16 (4%) have five and more children. Distributions related to educational status of children's of parents are presented between Table 3.27.–3.31.

Table 3.27. Distributions Related to Parents' First Child's Educational Status

1. Child's Educational Status	n	%
Do not go to school	80	19,6
Primary school	85	20,8
Secondary school	100	24,5
High school	96	23,5
University and higher	10	2,5
Other	4	0,9
Nonresponse	33	8,1
Total	408	100,0
Status of age appropriate ongoing education		
Yes	290	71,1
No	83	20,3
Nonresponse	35	8,6
Total	408	100

At Table 3.27., first child's educational status is examined and it is determined that, 100 (24.5%) of first children have secondary school, 96 (23.5%) have high school, 85 (20.8%) primary school, 10 (2.5%) of them seem to have education at universities and higher, 80 (19,6%) of them do not attend school. The parents who answered 'other' emphasize that their children continued in special education.

When the children's age and education level relationship is examined, 290 (71.1%) continued in an age appropriate education level, 83 (20.3%) of them do not continue in an age appropriate education level.

Table 3.28. The Distributions Related to Parents' Second Children's Educational Status

2. Child's Educational Status	n	%
Do not go to school	74	22,0
Primary school	92	27,4
Secondary school	68	20,2
High school	63	18,8
University and higher	6	1,8
Other	2	0,6
Nonresponse	31	9,2
Total	336	100

Status of Age Appropriate Ongoing Education	n	%
Yes	252	75,0
No	53	15,8
Nonresponse	31	9,2
Total	336	100

As seen in Table 3.28 the second child's learning situation is determined that, 92 (27.4%) of them go to primary school, 74 (22.0%) of them are not attending school, 68 (20.2%) go to secondary school, 63 (18.8%) go to high school, si (1.8%) of them stated university and higher. The 'other' responses stated that the children go to special education.

When children's age appropriate education status examined it is seen that 252 (75%) of them goes to an age appropriate education level, 53 (15,8%) do not go to an age appropriate education level.

Table 3.29. Distributions Related to Parents' Third Child's Educational Status

3. Child's Educational Status	n	%
Do not go to school	60	33,0
Primary school	51	28,0
Secondary school	33	18,1
High school	18	9,9
Nonresponse	20	11,1
Total	182	100
Status of Age Appropriate Ongoing Education		
Yes	128	70,3
No	34	18,6
Nonresponse	20	11,1
Total	182	100

When Table 3.29., is investigated it is determined that 60 (33,0%) of third children don't go to school, 51 (28,0%) of them attend primary school, 33 (18,1%) of them attend secondary school, 18 (9,9%) of them gets education at high school.

While it is determined that 128 (70,3%) of them gets an age appropriate education, 34 (%18,6) of them do not have an age appropriate education.

Table 3.30. Distributions Related to Parents' Fourth Child's Educational Status

4. Child's Educational Status	n	%
Do not go to school	24	34,8
Primary school	17	24,6
Secondary school	10	14,5
High school	6	8,8
University and higher	1	1,4
Other	1	1,4
Nonresponse	10	14,5
Total	69	100
Status of Age Appropriate Ongoing Education		
Yes	49	71,0
No	10	14,5
Nonresponse	10	14,5
Total	69	100

As seen in Table 3.30., it is determined that 24 (34.8%) children don't attend school, 17 (24.6%) of them primary school, 10 (14.5%) of them secondary schools, six (8.8%) of them high school, one (1.4%) child goes to university or higher education. The parents who stated the 'other' option stated that their children gets special education.

When examining the relationship between age and educational status it's seen that 49 (71.0%) of them gets an age appropriate education level, 10 (14.5%) of them do not have an age appropriate education.

Table 3.31. Distributions Related to Parents' Fifth and over Children's Educational Status

Five and More Children's Educational Status	n	%
Do not go to school	9	17,0
Primary school	8	15,0
Secondary school	2	3,8
Nonresponse	34	64,2
Total	53	100

Status of Age Appropriate Ongoing Education	n	%
Yes	14	26,4
No	5	9,4
Nonresponse	34	64,2
Total	53	100

When Table 3.31., is investigated it is seen that about five and more children that nine (17%) children do not go to school, eight (15.0%) of them goes to primary school, two (3.8%) of them goes to secondary school.

When the child's age and education levels are analyzed it is seen that 14 (26.4%) of them continued to their education level commensurate with their age, five (9,4%) of them do not continue their education level commensurate with their age.

Distributions related to parents' children who died after they were born is given in Table 3.32.

Table 3.32. Distributions Related to Parents' Children Who Died After Being Born

The Status of Child Died After Born	n	%
Yes	68	16,7
No	329	80,6
Nonresponse	11	2,7
Total	408	100,0

As seen in Table 3.32., it's determined that 68 (16.7%) parents have children died after the birth, 329 (80.6%) parents do not have a child who died after being born.

Table 3.33. Distributions Related to Health Checks of Women's and Their Baby's During Pregnancy and the Postpartum Period

Health Checks During the Pregnancy	n	%
Once a month	141	34,6
3–6 times	98	24,0
1–2 times	109	26,7
None	51	12,5
Nonresponse	9	2,2
Total	408	100,0

Baby's Health Check	n	%
Once month	169	41,4
Once in every 2–3 months	118	28,9
Once in every 4–8 months	74	18,1
Once in every 12 months	26	6,4
None	15	3,7
Nonresponse	6	1,5
Total	408	100,0
Having Regular Vaccine Done		
Yes	398	97,5
No	4	1,0
Nonresponse	6	1,5
Total	408	100,0
Taking Child to The Health Center During Health Problem		
Yes	378	92,6
No	23	5,6
Nonresponse	7	1,7
Total	408	100,0

When Table 3.33., is examined it is determined that 141 (34.6%) women get a monthly health check during the pregnancy period, 109 (26.7%) of them 1–2 times during the pregnancy period, 98 (24.0%) of them 3–6 times in the pregnancy period 51 (12.5%) of them never had a health check.

When babies' health check status is examined it is seen that 169 (41.4%) of them once in a month, 118 (28.9%) of them once in every 2–3 months, 74 (18.1%) of them once in every 4–8 months, 26 (6.4%) of them once in 12 months, 15 (3.7) do not appear to get a health check.

When the child's vaccine status is examined it is seen that 398 children (97.5%) of them have regular vaccine, four (1%) of them have not been regularly vaccinated.

378 (92.6%) parents stated that they take the child to the health center for health problems, 23 (5.6%) stated they do not.

Distribution of children's health insurance in households is given in Table 3.34.

Table 3.34. Distribution of Children's Health Insurance in Households

Children's Health Insurance Status	n	%
Yes	384	94,1
No	18	4,4
Nonresponse	6	1,5
Total	408	100,0
Children's Health Insurance Institution		
SSK	90	22,1
Bagkur	8	1,9
Pension fund	3	0,7
Greencard	283	69,4
Nonresponse	24	5,9
Total	408	100,0

As seen in Table 3.34., 384 (94.1%) of the children that were included in the survey benefit from health insurance. 18 (4.4%) of them lack health insurance.

When the institutions of health insurance of children in households were investigated, it was found that 283 (69.4%) of them have green cards, 90 (22.1%) of them have SSK, 8 (2.0%) of them have Bagkur, 3 (0.4%) of them have pension funding.

The distribution of health status of children in households is given in Table 3.35.

Table 3.35. Distribution of Health Status of Children in Households

The Status of a Significant Disease in Children	n	%
Yes	43	10,5
No	360	88,2
Unanswered	5	1,2
Total	408	100,0
The Status of An Undiagnosed Disease of Children		
Yes	27	6,6
No	364	89,2
Unanswered	17	4,2
Total	408	100,0

The Status of Presence of Disabled Children in Households	n	%
Yes	55	13,5
No	332	81,4
Nonresponse	21	5,1
Total	408	100,0

As seen in Table 3.35, it was found that 360 (88,2%) of children in households do not have a significant disease, whereas 43 (10.5%) of them have a significant disease. It was found that when undiagnosed health status of children was investigated, while 364 (89,2%) of them have no medical problem undiagnosed 27 (6.6%) of them have an undiagnosed medical problem 55 (13,5%) of parents of the children in the study have a disabled child.

Distribution of children's nutrition-related problems and number of meals in households is given in Table 3.36.

Table 3.36. Distribution of Children's Nutrition-Related Problems and Number of Meals in Households

Status of The Nutrition-Related Health Problems of Children	n	%
Yes	112	27,5
No	283	69,3
Nonresponse	13	3,2
Total	408	100
Number of Meals		
Three	284	69,6
Two	87	21,3
One	6	1,5
Four	14	3,4
Five	1	0,2
Nonresponse	16	3,9
Total	408	100,0

When children's nutrition-related problems was investigated in Table 3.36, 112 (27,5%) of children have health problems due to malnutrition, while 283(69,3%) was determined to have nutrition related problems.

When the number of meals children have was investigated, it was found that 284 (69.6%) have three meals, 87 (21.3%) have two meals, 14 (3.4%)

have four meals, six (1.5%) have one meal and one (0.2%) has five meals in a day.

The distribution of children starting primary school and having a pre-school education is given in Table 3.37.

Table 3.37. Distribution of Children in Households Starting Primary School and Having A Pre-School Education

Status for Starting Primary School on Time	n	%
Yes	349	85,5
No	21	5,1
Nonresponse	38	9,3
Total	408	100,0
Status for Having a Pre-School Education		
Yes	40	9,8
No	339	83,1
Nonresponse	29	7,1
Total	408	100,0
Duration of Pre-School Education		
0–1 year	37	92,5
2–3 year	2	5,0
4 years and over	1	2,5
Total	40	100,0

Table 3.37 shows that 349 (85,5%) of children in households started primary school on time, 21 (5.1%) of them did not start on time. It was also found that 339 (83,1%) of those children did not have a pre-school education and only 40 (9,8%) of them had a pre-school education.

When we analyzed the duration of the pre-school education for those who had a pre-school education, we found that 37 (92,5%) had less than one year, two (5%) had 2–3 years and one (2,5%) had more than four years.

The distribution of children continuing education on a regular basis is given in Table 3.38.

Table 3.38. *Distribution of Children Continuing Education on a Regular Basis*

Regular Attendance	n	%
Yes	344	84,3
No	18	4,4
Nonresponse	46	11,3
Total	408	100,0

As seen in Table 3.38, 344 (84,3%) children have regular attendance; whereas, 18 (4,4%) of them don't attend classes regularly.

Table 3.39 shows the status for discontinuation of compulsory education and reasons for it.

Table 3.39. *Distribution of Children and the Status for Discontinuation of Compulsory Education and Reasons for it*

Status for Discontinuation in Compulsory Education	n	%
Yes	31	7,6
No	323	79,2
Nonresponse	54	13,2
Total	408	100,0
Training Stage at Which Education was Ceased		
Not Attending Primary School	7	17,5
Not Attending Secondary School	6	15
Not Attending High School	27	67,5
Reasons for Discontinuation in Education		
Financial difficulties	15	35,7
Demotivation of children to study	20	47,6
Working	2	4,8
Other	5	11,9
Total	42	100

As seen in Table 3.39, it was found that the majority of children - 323 (79.2%) of them continue compulsory education and 31 (7.6%) of them do not. Within those who do not continue education, the training state where they stop attending the classes, is high school for 27 (67,5%) of them, primary school for seven (17.5%) and secondary school for six (15%) of them.

When a closer look was done for the cases in which children cannot proceed with their education, it was found that 20 (47.6%) of them do not want to continue going to school and study. 15 (35.7%) of them are unable to attend school due to financial constraints and two (4.8%) of them have a job and have stopped studying.

Table 3.40 shows the distribution on status of payment of education expenses by children's parents and the distribution on which items money is spent.

Table 3.40. Distribution on Status of Payment of Education Expenses by Children's Parents and on Which Items Money Is Spent

Status for Payment of Education Expenses by Parents	n	%
Yes	173	42,4
No	198	48,5
Nonresponse	37	9,1
Total	408	100,0
Money Spent Monthly for a Child's Education		
0 TL	72	17,6
1–100	179	43,9
101–300	103	25,2
301–500	8	2
501 and above	1	0,2
Nonresponse	45	11
Total	408	100
The Items Money was Spent on		
School allowance	144	24,7
Notebooks, books, stationery, etc.	194	33,3
Service fee	15	2,6
School fees	88	15,1
Clothes, etc.	48	8,2
Other	4	0,7
Nonresponse	90	15,4
Total	583	100

The 3.40 shows that 198 (48,5%) of the parents can not afford the education expenses and 173 (42,4%) of them can. 179 (43,9%) spend 1–100 TL monthly, 103 (25,2%) 101–300 TL monthly, eight (2%) 301–500 TL monthly, 1 (0,2%) 501 TL and more monthly, while 72 (17,6%) seem to have no expenditure. The money spent on children's education when examining results was 194 (33,3%) for a notebook, book, stationary, etc.

144 (24,7%) school allowance, 88 (15,1%) school fees, 48 (8,2%) clothes and etc, 15 (2,6%) seems to spend on service charges.

Distributions of status of external support that families receive to pay for the educational expenses and the source of this support is given in Table 3.41.

Table 3.41. Distribution of Status of External Support That Families Receive to Pay for the Educational Expenses and the Source of This Support

Status for Receiving an External Support	n	%
Yes	255	62,5
No	110	27,0
Unanswered	43	10,5
Total	408	100,0
Sources of the Support for Educational Needs of Children		
Family/Relatives	44	9,7
School	68	15
Social Assistance and Solidarity Foundation	187	41,2
Municipality	5	1,1
Foundations/Associations	8	1,8
Nonresponse	141	31,1
Total	453	100

As seen from the Table 3.41, 255 (62,5%) parents receive external support and 110 (27,0%) do not get any support for the educational expenses of their children, 187 (41,2%) parents receive support from Social Assistance and Solidarity Foundation, 68 (15%) from corresponding schools and, 44 (9,7%) from family and relatives.

The distribution of expectations of parents for their children about their future is given in Table 3.42.

Table 3.42. Distribution of Expectations of Parents for Their Children About Their Future

Expectations from Children	n	%
Study	394	96,6
Work	4	1,0
Nonresponse	10	2,5
Total	408	100,0
Reason Behind Expecting the Children Work Instead of Studying		
For that we need money	3	75
Profession to learn to have a job	1	25
Total	4	100,0
Contribution of Children's Education to Family's Economical Status		
Yes	394	96,6
No	5	1,2
Nonresponse	9	2,2
Total	408	100,0
The Type of Contribution of Children's Education to Family's Economical Status		
They can find a job easily and they have a profession	303	69,3
They can look after us (parents)	48	11
They will have knowledge	75	17,1
Nonresponse	11	2,5
Total	437	100

As shown in Table 3.42, 394 (96,6%) parents expect their children to continue their studies; whereas four (1%) expect their children to work. Within the four parents that expect their children to work, three (7,5%) specified the reason as they need money and the other (2,5%) indicated that their children can learn a skill while working. 394 (96,6%) of the parents when specifying education will contribute to the family, five (1,2%) indicate that education does not contribute to the family. Parents who indicated that they will contribute to the child's education; 303 (69,3%) did so because it would be easy to find a profession, 75 (17,1%) to become knowledgeable people, 48 (11%) of them have responded as their children will looks after them.

Distribution for the needs of children that parents cannot afford is given in Table 3.43.

Table 3.43. Distribution for the Needs of Children That Parents Cannot Afford

The Needs of Children That are not Met	n	%
Computer	190	21
Toy	98	10,8
Clothes	268	29,6
Food	188	20,7
Telephone	123	13,6
None	13	1,4
Medicine	11	1,2
Nonresponse	14	1,6
Total	905	100

As shown in Table 3.43., for children with unmet needs, 268 (29.6%) of them need children's clothes, 190 (21%) need for a computer, 188 (20.7%) need for children's food, 123 (13.6%) have phone needs, 98 (10.8%) need toys, 11 (1.2%) need for drugs, while 13 (1,4%) parents stated that there was no need.

Distribution for status for giving an allowance to children are presented in Table 3.44.

Table 3.44. Distribution for Status for Giving an Allowance to Children

Status for Giving Children an Allowance	n	%
Yes	201	49,3
No	194	47,5
Nonresponse	13	3,2
Total	408	100,0
The Amount of Money Given		
0–1	70	36
2–3	75	38,7
4–5	27	14
6–7	3	1,5
8 TL and over	19	9,8
Total	194	100

As seen in Table 3.44 it was determined that 201 (49.3%) children received an allowance and 194 (47.5%) did not. Parents stated that when examined the amount of money given to children was 75 (38.7%) received 2–3 TL, 70 (36%) 1 TL and less, 27 (14%) 4–5 TL, 19 (9.8%) 8 TL and above, three (1.5%) of them 6–7 TL.

Distribution of working children in the household are given in Table 3.45.

Table 3.45. The Distribution of the Children Working in the Household

Having a Working Child	n	%
Yes	9	2,2
No	386	94,6
Unanswered	13	3,2
Total	408	100,0
Jobs Children Work in		
Mechanic Works	3	33,3
Cafe/Restaurant Works	3	33,3
Market/Bazaar Works	1	11,1
Other	2	22,2
Total	9	100,0
The Age of Onset of A Child to Start Working		
4–7	1	11,1
12–15	1	11,1
16–19	7	77,7
Total	9	100,0
Child's Daily Working Hours		
0–3hrs	1	11,1
4–7hrs	1	11,1
8–11hrs	3	33,3
12hrs and above	4	44,4
Total	9	100,0
Child's Weekly Working Hours		
16–25hrs	2	22,2
36hrs and above	7	77,7
Total	9	100

Child's Working Rhythm	n	%
After school	1	11,1
Weekends	1	11,1
Everyday because the child doesn't attend school	7	77,7
Total	9	100,0
Child's Preference to Spend Money He Earns		
Supporting family	7	77,7
Taking the student loans	2	22,2
Total	9	100,0
Child Likes the Job		
Yes	8	88,8
No	1	11,1
Total	9	100,0
Child's Fear/Worry About the Job		
Yes	1	11,1
No	8	88,8
Total	9	100,0

As shown the Table 3.45., it was found that the majority of children - 386 (94,6%) do not work, but nine (2,2%) of them do work. Three (33,3%) of the children work in a repair shop, three (33,3%) of them work at a cafe/ restaurant, two (22,2%) of them work at different jobs, one (11,1%) worked in market/bazaar. It is seen that seven (77,7%) children are 16–19 years old, one (11,1%) is 12–15 years old, one (11,1%) is 4–7 years old.

Four (44,4%) children work daily more than 11 hours, three (33,3%) about 8–11 hours, one (11%) about 4–7 hours, one (11,1%) about 0–3 hours. When we analyse the working hours in a week, seven (77,7%) of them work weekly more than 36 hours, two (22,2%) about 16–25 hours. Seven (77,7%) work everyday because they don't go to school, one (11,1%) works only on the weekends, one (11,1%) work after school.

Seven (77.7%) children support their home with money received, while two (22.2%) of them spend money for school. Eight (88.8%) children love their work, while one (11.1%) child does not like his job. This one child works at the mechanic shop and his master acts badly towards him. It was found that eight (88,8%) children don't fear or feel sad when they work, while one (11,1%) child does.

The distribution showing the relationship of children with their friends and the time they can spend for playing are given in Table 3.46.

Table 3.46. The Distribution Showing the Relationship of Children with Their Friends and the Time They Can Spend for Playing

The Behavior of Child's Friends Towards the Child	n	%
Good	324	79,4
Bad	38	9,3
Nonresponse	46	11,3
Total	408	100,0
The Time the Child Spends on Playing		
Yes	298	73,0
No	83	20,3
Nonresponse	27	6,6
Total	408	100,0

As can be seen in Table 3.46, it was determined that 324 (79,4%) children in households have good relations with friends; whereas 38 (9,3%) have bad relations. When examined the children's play time is spent with 298 (73%) children spend time playing games, while 83 (20,3%) do not spend time playing.

The distribution regarding the situation of children in the household who do not come home is given in Table 3.47.

Table 3.47. Distribution Regarding the Situation of Children in the Household Who Do Not Come Home

The Situation When the Child Stays Outside	n	%
Yes	21	5,1
No	364	89,2
Nonresponse	23	5,6
Total	408	100,0
The Time Period When The Child Does Not Come Home Without Parents Knowing		
One day	4	19,1
A couple of days	4	19,1
A couple of weeks	1	4,7
Nonresponse	12	57,1
Total	21	100,0

As seen in Table 3.47 it was determined that 364 (89,2%) children do not show the behavior of absenteeism, and 21 (5,1%) of them remained in the street. It was found 4 children do not come home without their parents knowing (19,1%) for one day, four (19,1%) of them a couple of days, one (4,7%) child for one to two weeks.

Distribution of children in households have a friend living on the streets or working situation is given in Table 3.48.

Table 3.48. Distributions of Status of Children Having a Friend Who Lives/ Works on Street

Children having a Friend Living/Working on the Street	n	%
Yes	34	8,3
No	336	82,4
Nonresponse	38	9,3
Total	408	100,0

As seen in Table 3.4834 (8,3%) seem to have friends that are living or working on the street.and 336 (82,4%) do not.

Distribution showing number of children in households having bad habits and committing crimes are given in Table 3.49.

Table 3.49. Distribution Showing Number of Children in Households Having Bad Habits and Committing Crimes

Child Having a Bad Habit	n	%
Yes	62	15,2
No	322	78,9
Nonresponse	24	5,8
Total	408	100,0
Types of Child's Bad Habits		
Lying	31	33,7
Theft	4	4,3
Use of the volatiles	2	2,1
Smoking	36	39,2
Using alcohol	8	8,8
Running away from home	5	5,4
Other	6	6,5
Total	92	100

The Child Has a Previous Record of Crime	n	%
Yes	14	3,4
No	373	91,4
Nonresponse	21	5,1
Total	408	100,0
Punishment of the Child Due to the Crime Committed		
Yes	10	71,4
No	4	28,6
Total	14	100,0
The Attitude Towards Child's Bad Behavior		
We beat	57	11
We shout at the child	257	49,8
We ignore	17	3,3
We talk about the bad behavior	163	31,6
Other	7	1,4
Nonresponse	15	2,9
Total	516	100

As seen in Table 3.49.m it was determined that 322 (78,9%) children don't have bad habits; whereas 62 (15,2%) of them have bad habits. It was found that children who have bad habits, 36 (39.2%) of them smoke, 31 (33.7%) lie, eight (8.8%) use alcohol, five (5.4%) run away from home, four (4.3%) of them steal, two (2.1%) use the volatiles.

373 (91,4%) before the crime did not have a record, while 14 (3.4%) did. It was found that 10 (71.4%) of them received a punishment, four (28.6%) did not. 257 (49.8%) parents have shouted due to their child's bad behavior, 163 (31.6%) parents speak about the behaviour, 57 (11%) beating their, 17 (3.3%) of them ignore it.

Distribution relating to the situation of parents having children under protection or children adopted are given in Table 3.50.

Table 3.50. Distributions Relating to the Situation of Parents Having Children Under Protection or Children Adopted

Having the Child Adopted or Under Protection Status	n	%
Yes	6	1,5
No	392	96,1
Nonresponse	10	2,4
Total	408	100,0

As seen in Table 4.50, six (1,5%) parents have their child under the protection or have the child adopted, while 392 (96,1%) parents do not.

The distribution showing the situation when children have a private bedroom and toys belonging to themselves are given in the Table 3.51.

Table 3.51. Distribution Showing the Situation When Children Have a Private Bedroom and Toys Belonging to Themselves

The Child Has His Own Room	n	%
Yes	39	9,6
No	362	88,7
Nonresponse	7	1,7
Total	408	100,0
The Child Has His Own Toy to Play		
Yes	154	37,7
No	244	59,8
Nonresponse	10	2,5
Total	408	100,0

As seen in Table 3.51 it was found that 362 (88,7%) children in the household haven't their own room and 244 (59,8%) have no toys that are their own. It seems to be 39 (9,6%) have their own room and 154 (37,7%) of them have their own toy.

Distribution showing daily TV viewing time of children are given in Table 3.52.

Table 3.52. Distributions Showing Daily TV Viewing Time of Children

Child's Daily TV Viewing Time	n	%
1–2 hours	174	42,6
3–4 hours	156	38,2
5 or more hours	25	6,2
Nonresponse	53	13
Total	408	100

As seen in Table 3.52., it was determined that 174 (42.6%) children in the household watch 1–2 hours a day of TV, 156 (38.2%) 3–4 hours a day, 25 (6.2%) watch television five hours or more per day.

Distribution regarding the situation of children in the household having healthy diet are given in table 3.53.

Table 3.53. Distribution Regarding the Situation of Children in the Household Having Healthy Diet

Situation of have healty diet	n	%
Yes	68	16,7
No	335	82,1
Nonresponse	5	1,2
Total	408	100,0

As seen in Table 4.53 it was found that the majority of children' in the household, 335 (82,1%) of them do not have healthy diet, while 68 (16,7%) of them have a healthy diet.

Distributions of the children's unmet demand in the household is given in Table 3.54.

Table 3.54. Distribution on the Situation of Children's Unmet Demand

Being Unable to Meet The Child's Request	n	%
Yes	334	81,9
No	65	15,9
Nonresponse	9	2,2
Total	408	100,0

Having Difficulties to Meet Child's Requests	n	%
Food	146	18,9
Need For Education	88	11,4
Computer/Mobile Phone	211	27,4
Clothes	196	25,5
Travel/Vacation	39	5
Other	24	3,1
Nonresponse	67	8,7
Total	771	100
The Child's Response to Unmet Demand		
Crying/upset	194	38,8
Making comparisons	56	11,2
Sulking	60	12
Blame Us	39	7,8
Being understanding	83	16,6
Other	2	0,4
Nonresponse	66	13,2
Total	500	100

As seen in Table 3.54 mostly children in households, 334 (81.9%) of them there are unmet demands, while 65 (15.9%) of them do not. When examined children's unmet demands, 211 (27,4%) want a PC/mobile phone, 196 (25,5%) clothes, 146 (18,9%) food, 88 (11,4%) have needs related to education, 39 (5%) have travel demands. It was determined that unmet children respond with 194 (38,8%) crying or getting mad, 83 (16,6%) understand and figured out the situation, 60 (12%) are offended, 56 (11,2%) made comparisons, 39 (7,8%) of them blamed the parent.

The distribution will be concerned over the situation of children in the household are given in Table 3.55.

Table 3.55. Distributions Relating to Worries About the Child's Future Status in the Household

Worry about the Child's Future	n	%
Yes	323	79,2
No	58	14,2
Nonresponse	27	6,6
Total	408	100,0

Worried Situations	n	%
About education	210	48,1
About work	80	18,2
About security	43	9,9
Living and financial resources	32	7,5
About future	9	2
Related to bad habits	20	4,6
About the environment and bad friends	12	2,7
About health	15	3,4
About crime	3	0,7
About marriage	3	0,7
Total	437	100
The Definition of Poverty		
Neediness, poverty, etc	235	64
Hard or a bad thing	52	14,1
Helpless, Hopelessness unhappiness, etc	46	12,6
Unemployment	34	9,3
Total	367	100

As seen Table 3.55 it is found that the majority of children in the household, 323 (79,2%) of them said they worried about the future of their children to the parents. It was found that 210 (48,1%) of parents related by education, 80 (18,2%) related to the business, 43 (9,9%) related by security, 32 (7,5%) related by living and relevant financial resources, nine (2%) related by future, 20 (4,6%) related by bad habits, 12 (2,7%) related by environment and bad friends, 15 (3,4%) related by health, 10 (2,2%) related by loss of parent, three (0,7%) related by crime and three (0,7%) have marriage anxiety.

Finally the parents were asked for the definition of poverty. While 235 (64%) defined poverty as being penniless and neediness, 52 (14,1%) defined it as a difficult and a bad situation, 46 (12,6%) defined it with pessimistic feelings such as being hopeless and unhappiness. 34 (9,3%) of them described poverty as being unemployed.

3.3. Qualitative Findings of Interviews with Parents

This chapter includes information about questions asked to parent participants and their responses. Interviews were conducted with 20 adults within the scope of qualitative analysis and the obtained responses were analyzed through the MASQDA12 program which makes qualitative data analysis via a computer. Responses given to interview questions are analyzed as presented below.

"How can you define poverty?" Distribution of responses given to this question are presented in Figure 3.1.

Figure 3.1. Distribution of Definitions of Poverty by Parents

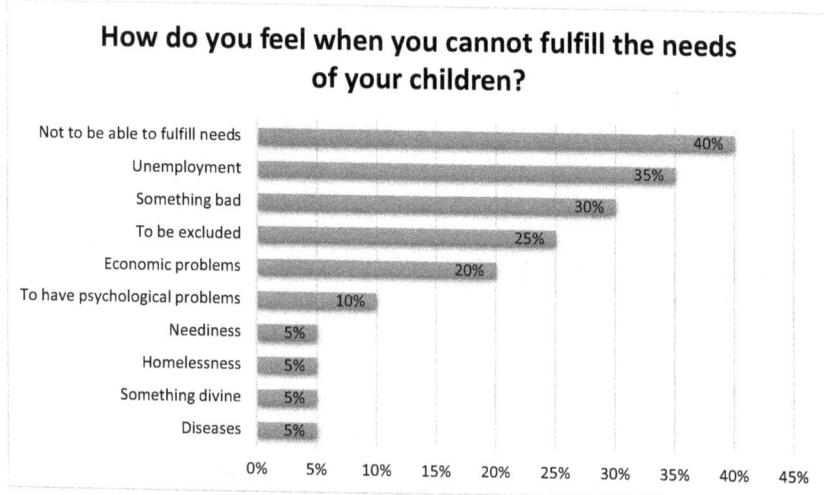

According to Figure 3.1., parents define poverty as; not to be able to meet needs (40%), unemployment (5%), something bad (30%), to be excluded (25%), economical problems (20%), to have psychological problems (10%), neediness (5%), homelessness (5%), something divine (5%), diseases (5%). Within the parents P5 responded to the question, "How can you define poverty?" as follows; "Poverty is something given by God. This life is a test. God grants poverty or welfare to anyone He wishes."

Distribution of responses given to question; "How do you spend a day?" are presented in Figure 3.2.

86

Figure 3.2. Distribution of How Parents Spent a Day

How do you spend a day?

Doing housework	78,9%
Visiting friends/neighbors	52,6%
Taking care of children	52,6%
Watching TV	26,3%
Shopping	21,1%
Praying	15,8%

0,0% 10,0% 20,0% 30,0% 40,0% 50,0% 60,0% 70,0% 80,0% 90,0%

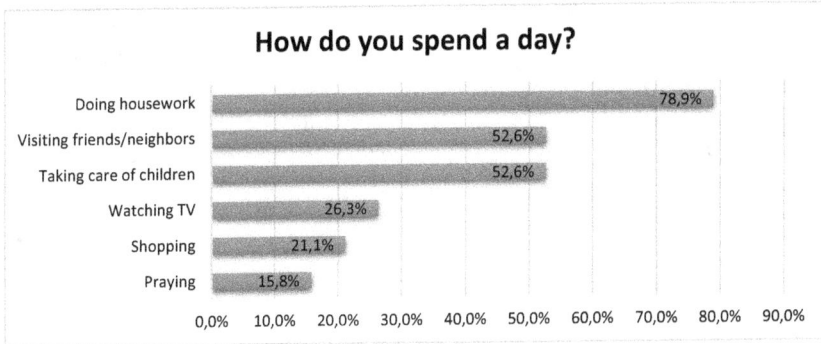

As is shown in Figure 3.2., the majority of parents are spending a day with, doing housework (78.9%), visiting friends/neighbors (52,6%), taking care of children (52,6%), watching tv (26,3%), and shopping (15.8%).

When parents asked if they get any aid apart from the foundation the majority (15%) stated that they do not get any aid apart from the foundation. It is seen that the rate of parents who get aid apart from the foundation is 15%. They stated that they are getting mainly food aid and these aids are given from Mamak Municipality or Metropolitan Municipality.

"What kind of needs of your children that you cannot meet?" Distribution of responses given to this question are presented in Figure 3.3.

Figure 3.3. Distribution of Needs of Children That Parents Cannot Meet

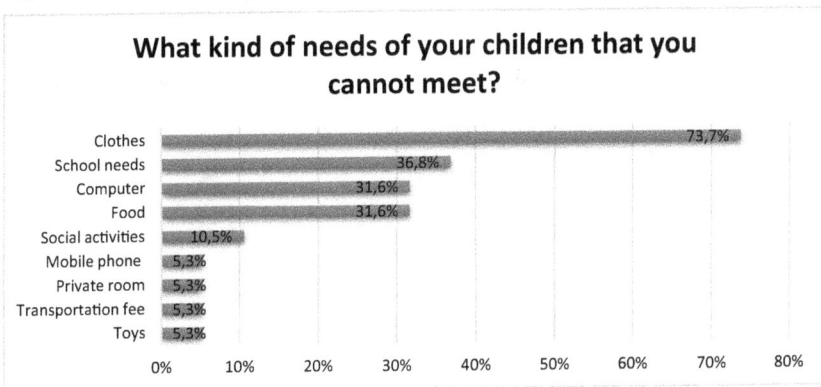

What kind of needs of your children that you cannot meet?

Clothes	73,7%
School needs	36,8%
Computer	31,6%
Food	31,6%
Social activities	10,5%
Mobile phone	5,3%
Private room	5,3%
Transportation fee	5,3%
Toys	5,3%

0%   10%   20%   30%   40%   50%   60%   70%   80%

87

As it shown in Figure 3.3., the majority of the parents (73,7%) cannot meet their children's clothing needs which is followed by school needs (36,8%), food (31,6%), computer (31,6%). Likewise the minority of the parents stated that they cannot meet their children's needs such as social activities, toys, transportation fees, private room and mobile phone.

"How do you feel when you cannot fulfill the needs of your children?" Distribution of Responses given to this question are presented in Figure 3.4.

Figure 3.4. Distribution of How Parents Feel When They Cannot Fulfill the Needs of Their Children

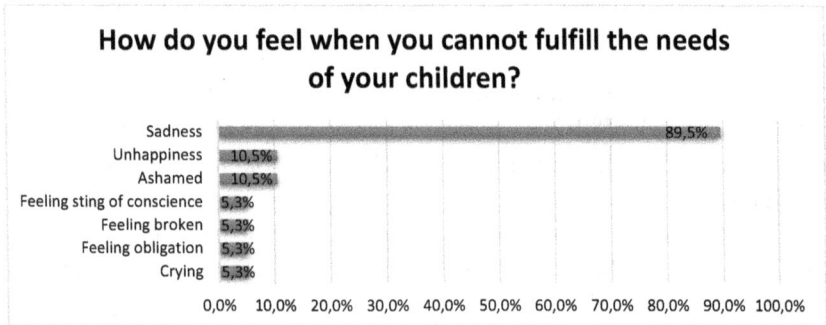

When Figure 3.4 is examined the majority of parents (89,5%) who cannot meet the needs of their children feel sadness, while a small part of parents feel ashamed, unhappiness, broken, obligation, sting of conscience and cry. One of the mothers (A6) responded question as *"I feel sad, I want him/her to eat and travel like others"*.

"Has your child ever been unable to continue education due to poverty?" Distribution of responses given to this question are presented in Figure 3.5.

Has your child ever been unable to continue education due to poverty?

No	50%
Yes	40%
Sometimes	5%

0%   10%   20%   30%   40%   50%   60%

When Figure 3.5 is examined, 40% of the parents' children are unable to continue education, some of the children who unable to continue education due to lack of transportation fee.

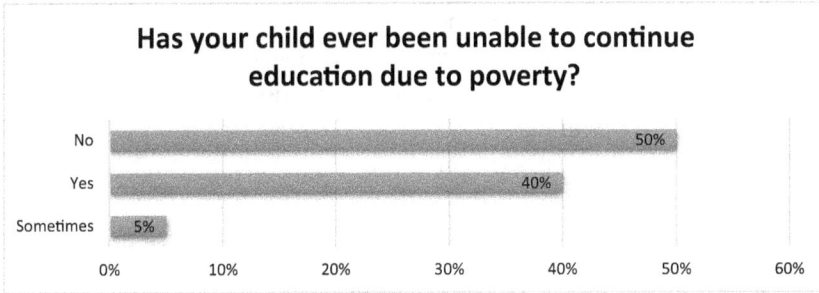

"What's your child's reaction when his/her school needs are not fulfilled?" Distribution responses given to this question are presented in Figure 3.6.

Figure 3.6. Distribution of Responses of Parents Whose Children's Reaction When His/Her School Needs Are Not Fulfilled

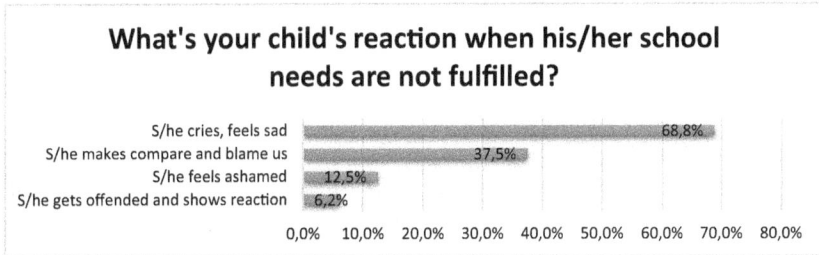

What's your child's reaction when his/her school needs are not fulfilled?

S/he cries, feels sad	68,8%
S/he makes compare and blame us	37,5%
S/he feels ashamed	12,5%
S/he gets offended and shows reaction	6,2%

0,0% 10,0% 20,0% 30,0% 40,0% 50,0% 60,0% 70,0% 80,0%

As shown in Figure 3.6., according to the parents when their children's school needs are not fulfilled their children often cry and feel sad (68,8%), 37,5% of them make comparisons and blame their parents. One of the parents (P18) responded to the question; "What's your child's reaction when his/her needs are not fulfilled?" as follows:

"I saw my daughter crying. She was sad that we would live in poverty one more month. She feels unhappy".

89

"Was there a problem with your child's health due to poverty?" While the majority of parents (66,7%) responding to this question "Yes, there was", 33,3% of them stated there was not any health problem due to poverty.

It is observed that 65% of the parents responded "Have ever been unable to buy medicine when you got sick?" question with yes, while 35% of them responded with no.

Majority of parents (90%) responded to "Do your children have enough nutrition?" question with "No".

"Where do you prefer for food shopping?" Responses given to this question are presented in Figure 3.7.

Figure 3.7. Distribution of Where Do Parents Prefer for Food Shopping

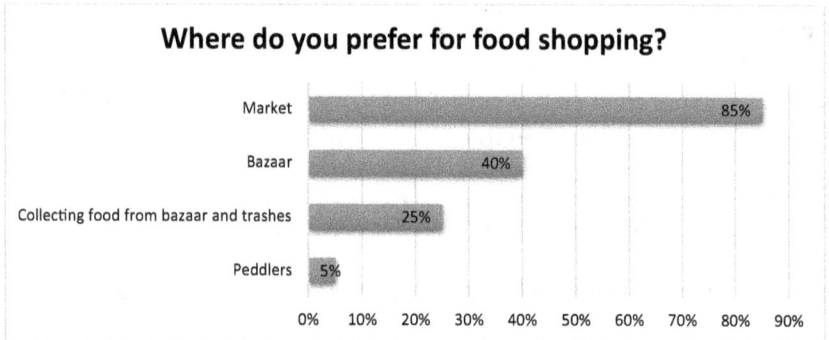

Where do you prefer for food shopping?

As shown in Figure 3.7., the majority of parents (85%) prefer markets for food shopping, while 40% of them prefer to buy from bazaar, 25% of the parents collect food from bazaar and trashes. Very few parents (5%) stated that they prefer to buy from peddlers. One of the parent P3 who collects food from bazaar and trashes responded as follows:

> "I collect from bazaar in late hours; I take whatever I find from the garbage. I buy overdue foods from market, so that I can buy cheap. Sometimes, I take from trashes".

"What kind of an environment would you like to live in if you had enough income?" Distribution responses given to this question are presented in Figure 3.8.

Figure 3.8. Distribution of Kind of Environments That Parents Like to Live In

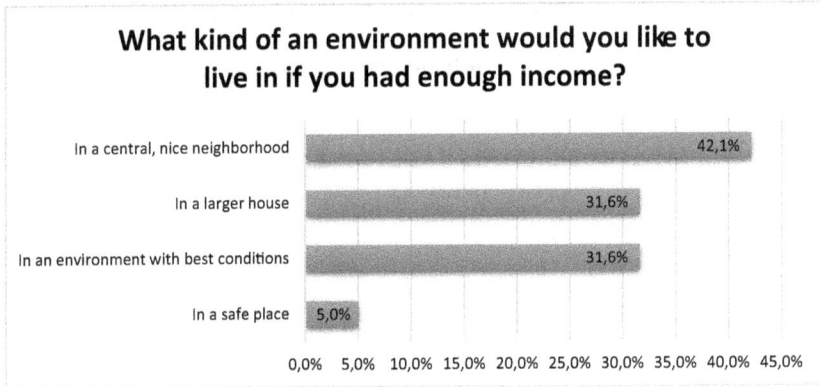

What kind of an environment would you like to live in if you had enough income?

In a central, nice neighborhood	42,1%
In a larger house	31,6%
In an environment with best conditions	31,6%
In a safe place	5,0%

0,0% 5,0% 10,0% 15,0% 20,0% 25,0% 30,0% 35,0% 40,0% 45,0%

As shown in Figure 3.8., 42,1% of the parents would like to live in a central, nice neighborhood, 31,6% of them would like to live in an environment with the best conditions, 31,6% of them would like to live in a larger house. "What are your concerns about future?" Distribution of Responses given to this question are presented in Figure 3.9.

Figure 3.9. Distribution of Parents' Concerns About Future

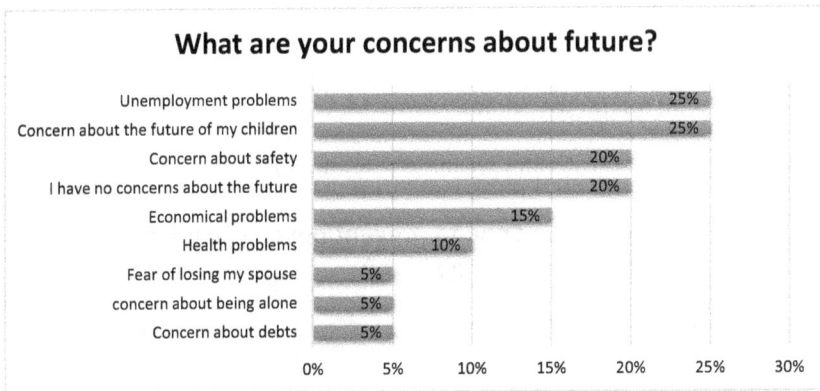

What are your concerns about future?

Unemployment problems	25%
Concern about the future of my children	25%
Concern about safety	20%
I have no concerns about the future	20%
Economical problems	15%
Health problems	10%
Fear of losing my spouse	5%
concern about being alone	5%
Concern about debts	5%

0% 5% 10% 15% 20% 25% 30%

When Figure 3.9. is examined, 25% of the parents had concerns about their children, which is followed by 25% unemployment, 20% safety, 15% economical problems. In addition 20% of the parents stated that they have no concerns about the future.

"What would you do if you had a magical wand?" Distributions of responses given to this question are presented in Figure 3.10.

Figure 3.10. Distributions of What Would Parents Do If They Had a Magical Wand

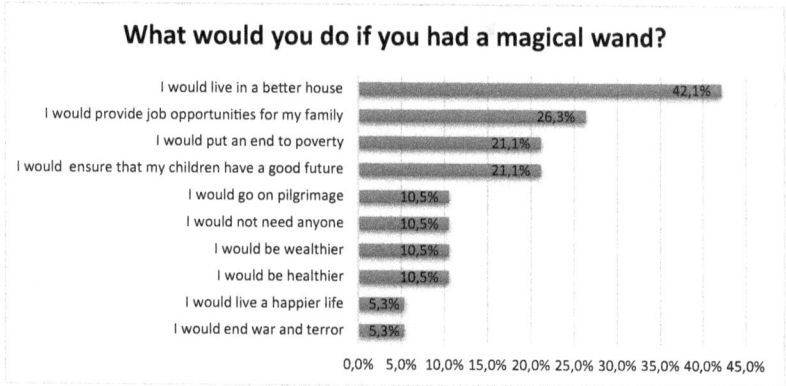

What would you do if you had a magical wand?

Response	Percentage
I would live in a better house	42,1%
I would provide job opportunities for my family	26,3%
I would put an end to poverty	21,1%
I would ensure that my children have a good future	21,1%
I would go on pilgrimage	10,5%
I would not need anyone	10,5%
I would be wealthier	10,5%
I would be healthier	10,5%
I would live a happier life	5,3%
I would end war and terror	5,3%

0,0% 5,0% 10,0% 15,0% 20,0% 25,0% 30,0% 35,0% 40,0% 45,0%

According to Figure 3.10., among the responses given to question; "What would you do if you had a magical wand?", "I would live in a better house" has the highest rate with 42.1% which is followed by 26,3%, "I would provide job opportunities for my family", 21,2% "I would put an end to poverty", 21,2% "I would ensure that my children have a good future". "What can be done to prevent poverty in your opinion?" Distribution of responses given to this question are presented in Figure 3.11.

Figure 3.11. Distributions of Opinions of Parents on Preventing Poverty

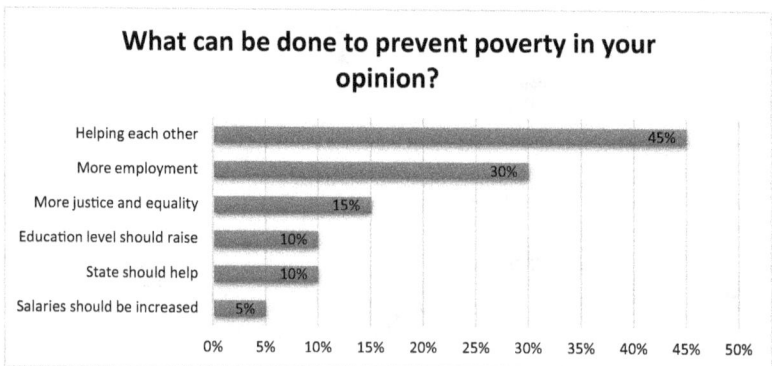

What can be done to prevent poverty in your opinion?

Response	Percentage
Helping each other	45%
More employment	30%
More justice and equality	15%
Education level should raise	10%
State should help	10%
Salaries should be increased	5%

0% 5% 10% 15% 20% 25% 30% 35% 40% 45% 50%

When Figure 3.11. is examined., among the responses given to question; "What can be done to prevent poverty in your opinion?", "helping each other" has the highest rate with 45% which is followed by 30% "more employment", while "salaries should be increased" has the lowest rate with 5%. One of the participants P17 responded to question; "What can be done to prevent poverty in your opinion?" as follows:

"Syrians started to come here, and everything started to get worse. In past, we used to receive a lot of aid. The prior duty of state is to take care of its own citizens". Another participant said (P5) *"People must work and shouldn't want more than rightful share. They should settle with what they have. Poverty stems from the greed of other people."*

"What would you change about yourself?" Distributions of responses given to this question are presented in Figure 3.12.

Figure 3.12. Distributions of What Would Parents Change About Themselves

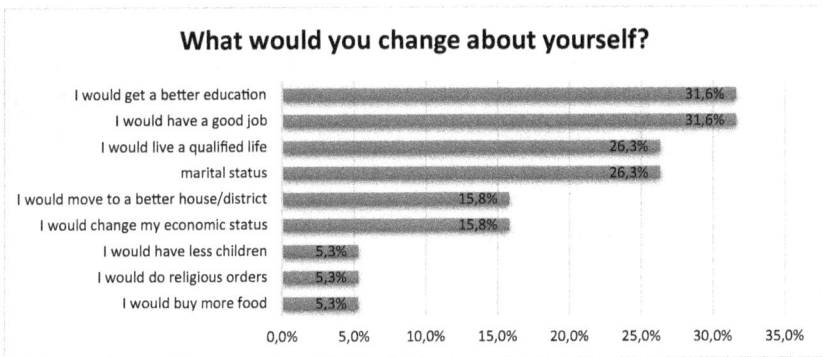

What would you change about yourself?

I would get a better education	31,6%
I would have a good job	31,6%
I would live a qualified life	26,3%
marital status	26,3%
I would move to a better house/district	15,8%
I would change my economic status	15,8%
I would have less children	5,3%
I would do religious orders	5,3%
I would buy more food	5,3%

When Figure 3.12. is examined, among responses given to question; "What would you change about yourself?", 31,6% of the parents responded as my job, while others answered 31,6% education status, 26,3% marital status, 26,3% life status, 15,8% economic status, 15,8% house.

One of the parents P19 responded question; "What would you change about yourself?" as follows;

"I wouldn't want any child. I wouldn't want to marry either. I haven't lived any peaceful day."

"What would you change about society?" Distributions of responses given to this question are presented in Figure 3.13.

Figure 3.13. Distributions of What Would Parents Change About Society

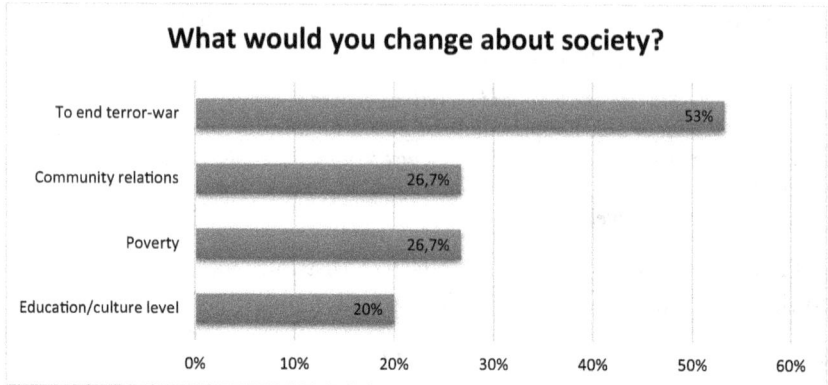

What would you change about society?

Category	Percentage
To end terror-war	53%
Community relations	26,7%
Poverty	26,7%
Education/culture level	20%

When Figure 3.13. is examined, among the responses given to question; "What would you change about society?", 53,3% of the parents want to end terror-war, 26,7% of the parents want to put an end to poverty. Rate of the parents who want to change education/culture level is 20%.

One of the parents P10 responded question; "What would you change about society?" as follows:

"If I received education, I would employ people around me and make them useful people for society. I would enable them to stand on their own legs. We have become introvert because of poverty".

3.4. Qualitative Findings of Interviews with Children

This chapter includes information about questions asked to child participants and their responses. Interview were conducted with 20 children within the scope of qualitative analysis and the obtained responses were analyzed through the MASQDA12 program which makes qualitative data analysis via a computer. Responses given to interview questions are analyzed as presented below.

"Are there any poor people around you? Can you define 'poverty' for me?" Distribution of responses given for these questions are presented in Figure 3.14.

Figure 3.14. Distribution of Definitions of Poverty Given by Children

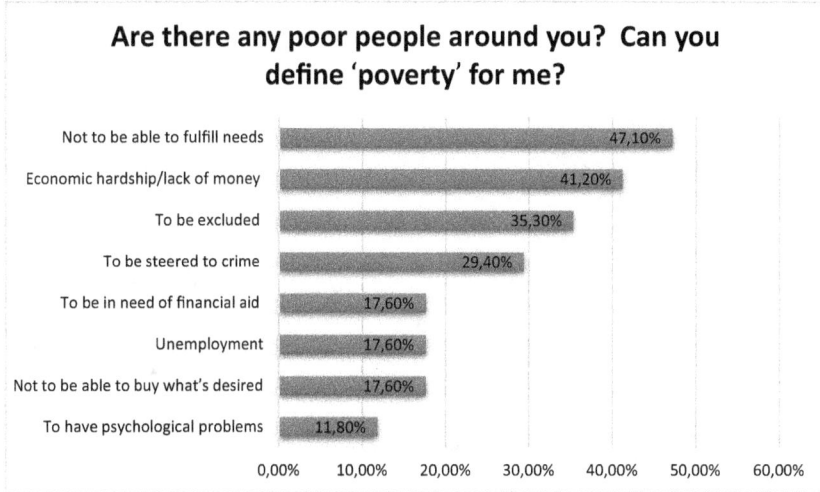

Are there any poor people around you? Can you define 'poverty' for me?

Category	Percentage
Not to be able to fulfill needs	47,10%
Economic hardship/lack of money	41,20%
To be excluded	35,30%
To be steered to crime	29,40%
To be in need of financial aid	17,60%
Unemployment	17,60%
Not to be able to buy what's desired	17,60%
To have psychological problems	11,80%

As presented in Figure 3.14, among the responses given to questions "Are there any poor people around you? Can you define 'poverty' for me?", all of the children responded that there is poor people around me and in definitions of poverty not to be able to fulfill needs has the highest rate with 47.1% which is followed by economic hardship/lack of money with 41.2%, to be excluded with 35.3%, to be steered to crime with 29.4%, not to be able to buy what's desired, unemployment and to be in need of financial aid with 1.7.6% and to have psychological problems with 11.8%. Within the children C1, C4 and C11 defined poverty as follows:

"Yes, there are. To wear torn clothes, not to be able to buy school needs, not to be able to go somewhere urgently... Not to be able to go to hospital when one's sick, if there is no money to take a bus (C1)." "Poverty is such a bad thing. May God protect everyone from it. Because there are really very poor people around us and they present a bad image of our environment due to poverty. Those in need of money, shoes... They become thieves and sell drugs. Actually, we have a very good place but some people do not know how to use this place and bring harm to it. I'm really ashamed of living in here sometimes. Our families started to live here because

of poverty. I hope from God that we'll be away from this place (C4)." "Yes, there are. In my opinion, poor people cannot buy food and clothes and do not have a house to live in. Those are people who are in need of financial aid and cannot buy something for their children, cannot meet their needs (C11)."

"What sort of things you cannot buy even though you want?" Distribution of responses to this question are presented in Figure 3.15.

Figure 3.15. Distribution of Things That Children Cannot Buy Even Though They Want

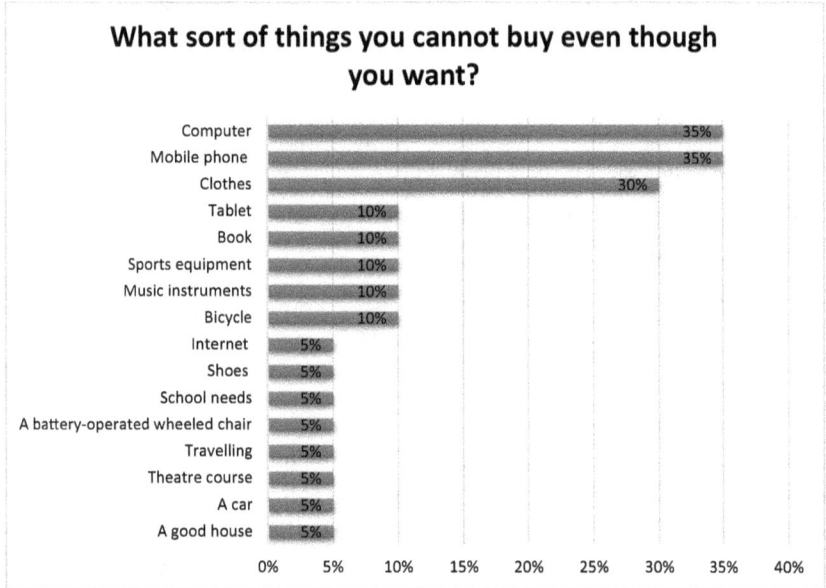

What sort of things you cannot buy even though you want?

Category	Percentage
Computer	35%
Mobile phone	35%
Clothes	30%
Tablet	10%
Book	10%
Sports equipment	10%
Music instruments	10%
Bicycle	10%
Internet	5%
Shoes	5%
School needs	5%
A battery-operated wheeled chair	5%
Travelling	5%
Theatre course	5%
A car	5%
A good house	5%

Figure 3.15. presents that there are many things that children cannot afford even though they ask for. Of these responses, a computer and mobile phone has the highest rate with 35% which is followed by clothes with 30%. In addition, children stated that they cannot afford bicycle, music instruments, sports equipment, book and tablet with 10%; a good house, a car, theatre course, travel, a battery-operated wheeled chair, school needs, shoes and internet with 5%. The rate of children who stated there is nothing that they cannot afford is 20% and the rate of those who stated they cannot afford anything is 5%. Within the children C6, C19 and C8 responded the

question; "What sort of things you cannot buy even though you want?" as follows:

> *"We cannot afford many things even though I ask for them. I do not want to force my family. I do not want to make them upset; I cannot buy a phone or needed clothes (C6)." "I wish to have clothes, phone, shoes and a luxury car. I wish to have a house with beautiful furniture (C19)." "Yes, there are. Computer, internet, tablet, bicycle, phone, clothes (C8)."*

"How do you feel when you cannot afford things that you ask for?" Distribution of responses given for this question are presented in Figure 3.16.

Figure 3.16. Distribution of Children's Feelings When They Cannot Afford Things That They Ask For

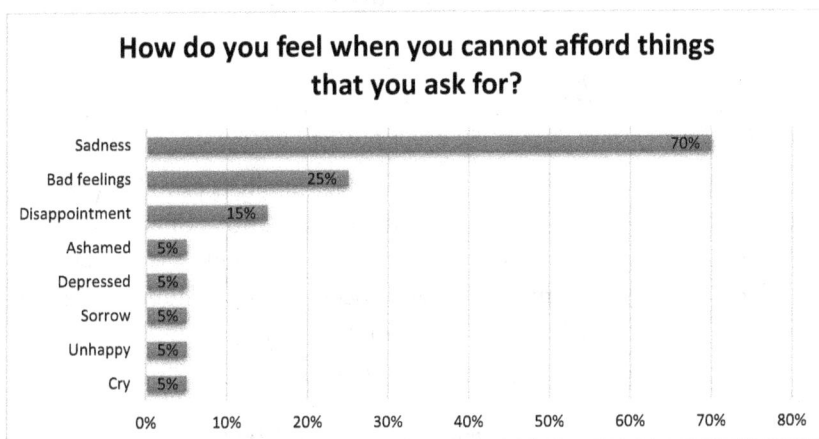

How do you feel when you cannot afford things that you ask for?

Feeling	Percentage
Sadness	70%
Bad feelings	25%
Disappointment	15%
Ashamed	5%
Depressed	5%
Sorrow	5%
Unhappy	5%
Cry	5%

Figure 3.16 presents the responses given to question; "How do you feel when you cannot afford things that you ask for?". Accordingly, 70% of children feel sadness; 25% feel bad and 15% feel disappointment. In addition, the rate of each responses "I cry", "I feel unhappy", "I feel sorrow", "I feel depressed", "I feel ashamed" is 5%. 10% of children stated that they do not feel anything. Within the children C4, C6 and C9 explained their thoughts on feelings when they cannot afford things that they ask for as follows:

> *"When I cannot buy things that I want, I feel sad without reflecting it to my family. I sometimes cry but I do not mind. I forget it in time. There are people in worse conditions, I'm thankful for our condition (C4)." "In fact, I feel sad just like any child, but there is nothing to do. I just say 'whatever...'. But I feel bad*

97

inside. I feel resentment (C6)." "I feel offended. I make effort to buy anything I want and I feel sorrow (C9)."

When the question of "Do you argue with your family about money?" was asked to the children the majority (65%) responded that they argue and within the children C12 and C4 explained their thoughts as follows:

"Yes, I argue with them from time to time. Because, they cannot give me even 1 Turkish lira. Financial situation is not important but living is hard (C12)." "Yes, I sometimes argue. I cannot tell them anything. But, after a while, I get ill-tempered. Sometimes, I say to myself; "Why don't I have? Why not me?". I ask such silly questions but then I ask to myself "Would my family want us to be like that?". Of course, they wouldn't. But, it happens (C4)".

Within the children who don't argue with their parents (35%) C5 and C6 explained their thoughts as follows:

"No. Because I know financial situation of my family. I wouldn't ask more than we could afford (C5)." "I mean, I wouldn't argue. Because they do everything they can. I do not get mad at them. If money is not enough, this is not their fault (C6)."

When pocket money given to children by their family is examined the majority (80%) take pocket money from their family; 40% of children think that their pocket money is satisfactory while 40% think it is not satisfactory. 20% of children do not receive any pocket money. Within the children C12 and C14 explained their thoughts on pocket money as follows:

"I do not receive pocket money regularly. Even if I do, it is not satisfactory. Therefore, I feel jealous of my friends from time to time (C12)." "They always give and it is enough for me, I'm proud of my family (C14)."

"How do you spend your pocket money given by your family?" Distribution responses given for this question are presented in Figure 3.17.

How do you spend your pocket money given by your family?

Canteen	50%
School expenditures	30%
Save their pocket money	25%
Market	15%
Do not have any pocket money	15%
Entertainment	10%
Personal needs	10%

(0%   10%   20%   30%   40%   50%   60%)

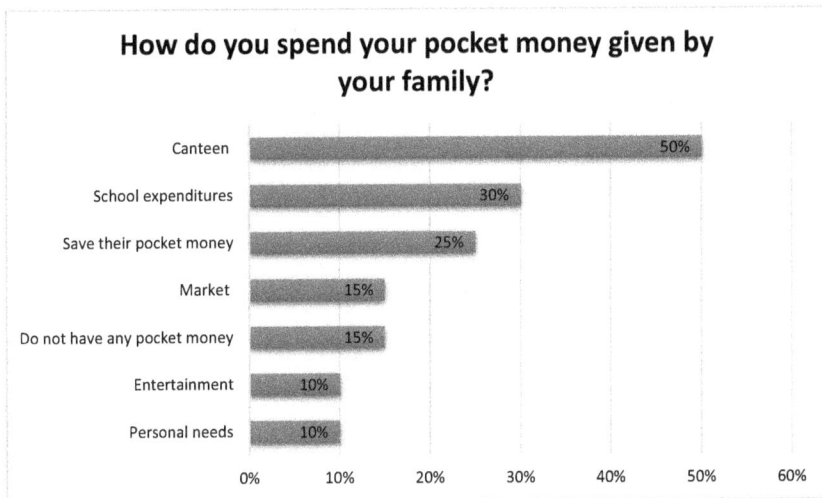

According to Figure 3.17., children most commonly use their pocket money for their food needs from canteen with the rate of 50%. In addition, it can be seen that children use 30% of their pocket money for their school expenditures, 15% for food needs from market and 10% for personal needs and entertainment. 25% of children can save their pocket money, yet 15% do not have any pocket money. Within the children C16, C10 and C6 explained their thoughts on how they spend pocket money given by their family as follows:

"If I'm hungry, I buy food; If I'm not hungry, I save the money or buy book or donate it (16)" "I buy food at lunch break at school (C10)." "In general, I spend a little and I save the rest, I buy school needs (C6)."

When question of "Do you share your pocket money with your friends?" was asked to the children the majority (70%) stated that they are sharing, 30% of them stated that they are not sharing their pocket money with their friends. Within the children C12, C14 and C16 explained their thoughts as follows:

"Yes. I share with my friend. S/he also shares with me (C12)." "Yes, his/her father is in prison. His/her mother has brain tumor. So, I share all my money with my friend (C14)." "Yes, I share my money in school back of the beyond. I do not

want to offend him/her (C16)." "No, they have a better financial condition than I have (C17)."

Likewise when question of "Do you share your food with your friends?" was asked to the children the majority (95%) stated that they are sharing their food with their friends. Within the children C16 and C12 explained their thoughts as follows:

> *"I mostly share, because I cannot stand seeing them in lack of food. Thank God, I always have even a little. I think that I might have been in their situation (C16)."*
> *Yes, I share with my friend. S/he also shares with me (C12)."*

"How do you feel when you see that your friends have what you ask for?" Distribution of responses given to this question are presented in Figure 3.18.

Figure 3.18. Distribution of Responses Given to Question; "How Do You Feel When You See That Your Friends Have What You Ask For?"

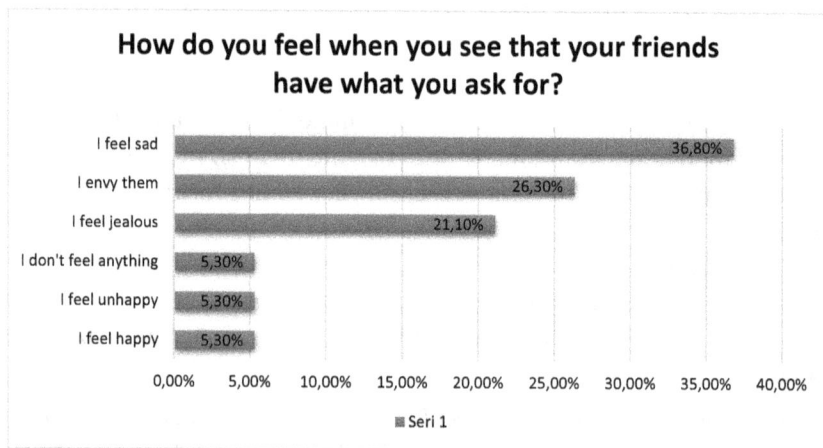

How do you feel when you see that your friends have what you ask for?

I feel sad	36,80%
I envy them	26,30%
I feel jealous	21,10%
I don't feel anything	5,30%
I feel unhappy	5,30%
I feel happy	5,30%

0,00% 5,00% 10,00% 15,00% 20,00% 25,00% 30,00% 35,00% 40,00%

■ Seri 1

According to Figure 3.18., responses given to this question; "How do you feel when you see that your friends have what you ask for?", the highest rate was found for "I feel sad" with 36.8%. Other responses include "I feel jealous, I want them too." "I envy them", "I feel happy", "I feel unhappy" and "I don't feel anything". Responses of the children C5 and C12 to question; "How do you feel when you see that your friends have what you ask for?" are presented as follows:

I feel jealous. At first, I feel very sad. But then, I get used to it. Then I don't mind it. Because, being happy is not all about things (C5)." "I feel jealous, I just wish that I can have these things one day. (C12)"

The majority of children (55%) in the study responded to the question of "Can you meet your school needs?" that they can meet their school needs, 45% of the children do not meet their school needs. C14 who stated that s/he can meet his/her school needs explained his/her thoughts as *"Yes I can and I feel very happy. I do not have to ask anything from my friends, so I don't become a subject of gossip for them.".* 82% of children stated to feel sad and 16% stated to feel helpless when they cannot meet their school needs. C3 and C1 who stated that they cannot meet their school needs explained their thoughts as follows:

"No. Therefore, I receive education from open high school. I can't even afford travel expenses (C3)." "No. I feel sad, I cannot catch up with lectures (C1)."

When the question of "How do school principal or teachers behave when you cannot meet your school needs?" was asked to the children, they responded to this question that the school principal or teachers have tolerance to children who cannot meet their school needs with the rate of 65%; however they show reaction with anger with the rate of 35%. Within the children C1 and C17 explained their thoughts as follows:

"Teacher doesn't get angry. However, I cannot buy a test book for instance. The principal says 'If you can't afford it, why do you come to school?' (C1)". "They get angry, they offend me in front of my friends, they say; 'If you don't have a uniform, notebook, what are you doing at school?' (C17)." "Our teachers and principal are very kind, they don't get angry (C13)."

When questions of "Do you see a doctor when you get sick?" "Can you buy the medicine prescribed by doctor?" was asked to the children, 75% of children have a health control and buy medicine when they get sick, yet 25% cannot go to hospital.

"When I get sick, I pretend to be fine (C4)." "Yes, I do. But transportation is a bit challenging. Because there is no hospital where I live. I buy medicine as far as we can afford (C9)."

"Which profession would you like to choose?" Distribution of responses to this question are presented in Figure 3.19.

Figure 3.19. Distribution Professions That Children Would Like to Choose

Which profession would you like to choose?

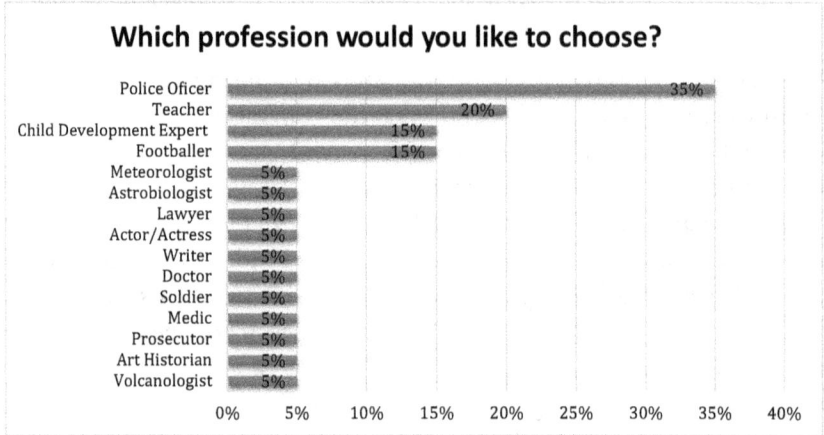

According to Figure 3.19., children prefer many different profession groups. Children want to be police officer mostly with the rate of 35%, teacher with the rate of 20% and child development expert and footballer with the rate of 15%. Responses of the children C4, C6 and C5 to question; "Which profession would you like to choose?" are presented as follows:

> "My biggest dream is to receive education on child development. This is what I want most. I hope that I can achieve. The reason why I want to choose this profession is that I couldn't go to kindergarten even though I wanted so much. I hope from God that I'll be able to (C4)." "I want to be a doctor. A child's doctor. To heal the children of poor families (C6)." "My biggest dream is to be a writer or theatre player. I believe that I'm talented in this (C5)."

"What would you do if you had a magical wand? Distribution responses given to this question are presented in Figure 3.20.

Figure 3.20. Distributions of What Would Children Do If They Had a Magical Wand

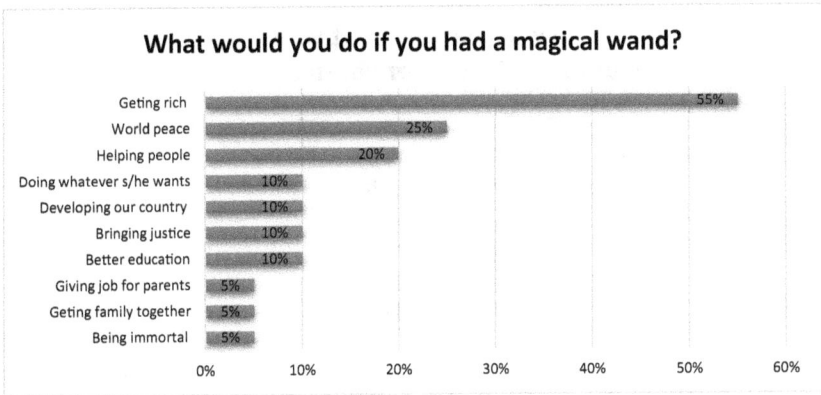

What would you do if you had a magical wand?

Category	Percentage
Geting rich	55%
World peace	25%
Helping people	20%
Doing whatever s/he wants	10%
Developing our country	10%
Bringing justice	10%
Better education	10%
Giving job for parents	5%
Geting family together	5%
Being immortal	5%

According to Figure 3.20., when responses given to question; "What would you do if you had a magical wand?" are examined, children reported that they have many wishes such as to get rich which has the highest rate of 55%, then world peace, helping people, developing our country and bringing justice. Responses of the children C12 and C20 to question; "What would you do if you had a magical wand? are presented as follows:

"At first, I wish peace, serenity and happiness for the world. I wish my family and everyone to be immortal. I wish the financial status of our family to be good; I wish my brother/sister could stand up (C12)." "I would make our martyr soldiers meet their families. I would want the war to end. I would help the poor (C20)."

"What would you change about yourself and your family if you were born again?" Distributions of responses given to this question are presented in Figure 3.21.

Figure 3.21. Distributions of What Children Want to Change About Themselves and Their Family

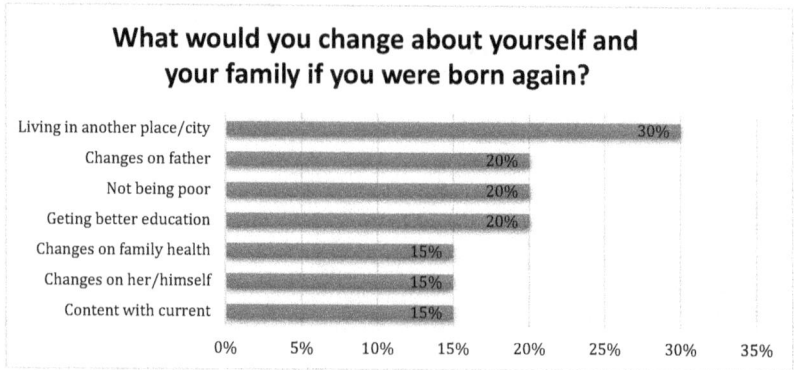

What would you change about yourself and your family if you were born again?

Living in another place/city	30%
Changes on father	20%
Not being poor	20%
Geting better education	20%
Changes on family health	15%
Changes on her/himself	15%
Content with current	15%

0%   5%   10%   15%   20%   25%   30%   35%

According to Figure 3.21., 40% of the children stated that they would want to not be poor and get a better education, 30% of the children stated that they would want to live in another place/city. Responses of the children C16 and C13 to question; "What would you do if you had a magical wand?" are presented as follows:

> "If I were born again, I would want my father and mother to get back together. I would want a good life, to live in better places and to forget about our problems (C16)." "I wouldn't change anything. I love my family so much. They do everything for me. They are very valuable (C13)."

"What would you change about society if you were born again?" Distributions of responses given to this question are presented in Figure 3.22.

Figure 3.22. Distributions of What Children Would Change About Society

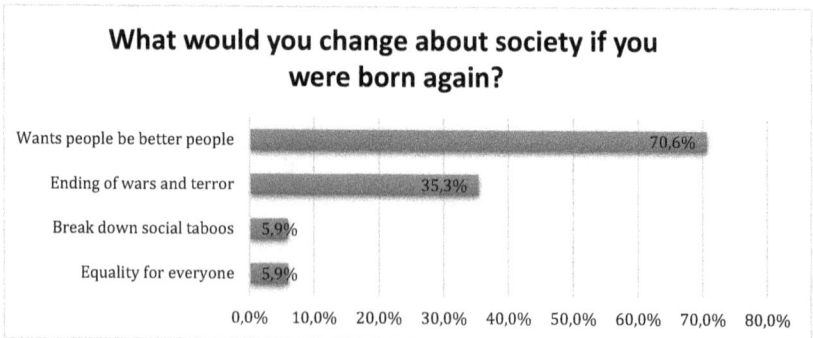

What would you change about society if you were born again?

Wants people be better people	70,6%
Ending of wars and terror	35,3%
Break down social taboos	5,9%
Equality for everyone	5,9%

0,0%   10,0%   20,0%   30,0%   40,0%   50,0%   60,0%   70,0%   80,0%

According to Figure 3.22, children want people not to be bad and to be better people most commonly with the rate of 70%. In addition, 35% of children stated that they want wars and terror to end. Within the children C12 and C1 stated what they would change about society as follows:

"Society is very cruel. I would want to steer them to happiness and peace. I would prevent financial hardship of society (C12)." "I would want people to be good, not to interfere in others' business and not to be aggressive (C1)."

4. Discussion

In this study, which is conducted for Mapping Child Poverty in Mamak District of Ankara, data about how people who applied to Mamak District Social Assistance and Solidarity Foundation and people who earned social aid lived poverty, data on how and to what degree children were affected by poverty were evaluated and analyzed. Of the population examined, data included parents' ages and marital status, information about the homes they are living in, children's ages, gender and educational status, children's state of health and children's occupational status.

In this research, most parts of which were conducted by home visits, it was seen that, although fathers were also present at the time of the visits, the majority of the participators of the survey were mothers (82,6%). Fathers were often observed to have directed the conductor(s) to mothers. Deduction was drawn that this attitude was most probably the sign of mothers' having more knowledge about their children than fathers, or fathers' lower interest in such surveys.

Information about participating families' marital status was accessed in the study. About the marital status, the most dramatic data was the divorce rate. According to the findings of the study 7,2% of fathers and 20,6% of mothers reported that they were divorced. Of those who were divorced, the majority connoted the cause as physical violence, others showed financial problems and bad habits such as substance addiction as the reason, while the divorce rate caused from affairs with someone other than the spouse was also significant. According to another study conducted by Ceren (2013), 50% of the families reported to have divorced due to financial problems, while 10% had declared the cause of divorce as violence. According to Ankara Development Agency's data, the number of divorced people is 22.166 as of 2012. In the length of time new poverty types arise and these may sometimes involve divorces (Durgun, 2011). Divorce generally causes financial problems. On occasions where the woman cannot receive maintenance allowance from her ex-husband it may cause financial problems and result in poverty risk (Öztürk & Çetin, 2009). Particularly woman's poverty means the child will result in poverty.

It was seen in the study that almost half of the fathers and one-third of the mothers had migrated to where they currently live from another settlement. More than half of the fathers who had migrated said the change in residence was due to the opportunity of employment, while more than half of the mothers mentioned health problems as the main migration cause.

According to Öztürk (2008), poor economic conditions in Turkey and disordered and even sometimes compulsory migration to cities from rural areas create negative results for children like early matrimony, child labor, juvenile delinquency and children's need for protection. Öztürk's study (2008) showed that 83,2% of the families experienced migration. Of the families migrated, 37,7% had stated the main reason as financial problems and unemployment, while 26,3% said they migrated for richer educational and health services of urban settlements. Erkan and Bağlı (2005)'s study showed that, of the migrated families, 21,5% had moved to cities to find a job. Öztürk's and Erkan and Bağlı's studies' findings are consistent with our study's results. Massive migration that occurred from the early 1980's had dominantly shaped the socio-cultural, economic and psychological structure of Turkish public (Gün and Bayraktar, 2008). Bilgin (2009) added that emigrational status should be carefully examined in relation with children's working status out on the streets. Bilgin concluded that 81,8% of the working children's families migrated to urban areas in the near past. It can be clearly observed that this ratio decisively affects child labor and child poverty.

Examining the financial liabilities and other debts of the participators of the study, it was revealed that the great majority had some form of debt. Of the debtors, almost half of them had liabilities of at least 5.000 TL or more, more than half of which stated they owed to banks. Kocatepe's 2011 study revealed that individuals' debt ratio was 42%. Ertürk's (2010) study showed that 85,6% of the participators had debt, 27,3% of which had loans over 3.000 TL. Not only the poor can be said to have loans, but medium and high class also sometimes prefer borrowing. But, while medium-high class has more ability to return their payments, those who receive financial/social aid are likely to experience more problems in paying back due to low and instable income, resulting in the deepening of their debt (Ertürk, 2010). Bakırtaş's study (2012) also revealed that, of the households included in the research, 61,4% had debts and 28,3% of the payment of loans had caused an overload on the family budget. 26,8% expressed that they had spent their income for debt payments. This, for us, brings into sharp relief of a vicious cycle, that is, individuals continuously borrow to continue their living and spent most of their income for back payments.

According to the Ministry of Public Works and Settlement's 2009 report, households had problems in receiving some public services such as natural gas due to failure of payment, because families meet their daily requirements by credit cards and are plunged into debt. The poor cannot provide themselves their daily necessities due to low income and thus have to borrow in some kind of way for food, shelter, education, etc. Although borrowing from individuals or retailers is also existent, the majority of the debt is in the form of bank loans, resulting in another threat, debt enforcement due to default credits. Thus some negative social – personal outcomes emerge, the most common of the social negative outcomes being the child labor.

The vast majority of the participators reported that they did not have an occupation. Almost half of the participators who have a job are daily servants, an occupation chosen mostly for its ease of accessibility, impermanency and mother's having capabilities only for this kind of job. According to Öztürk's study (2008) 65% of the participators were found to have a job, 87,2% of which had instable occupations. Of the participators 47,3% were employed in construction and 14,7% were housemaids. The low rate of employment might be annotated as the main reason for child labor. Inconsistent employment, employment contracts without specified intervals, wages even under base wage rate and irregular income are major factors of poverty. The uncertainty caused by irregular employment is thought to have negative effects on confidence (Öztürk, 2008). TurkStat reported that overall unemployment as of January 2016 in Turkey was 11,1%. Considering workforce and employment rates in Turkey, workforce over 15 years old accounts for 44,5% of total population, while the rate of 15 year olds' accession to workforce is 49,4% (UNDP, 2015).

Nearly half of the participators reported that they had been unemployed for at least three years, and 68,4% stated they were looking for an opportunity to have a job with regular income. Though these two figures might seem paradoxical, one should bear in mind that most participators were mothers, and child care and family household are perceived mainly as mothers' responsibility. Almost half of those who did not want to work stated they did not have a backup to look after their children. 21,7% also reported that their spouses did not want them to have a job, which might be conceived as a repercussion of Turkey's socio-cultural structure.

Evaluating the qualitative interview findings held with unemployed mothers, it has been found that mothers spent most of their days doing housework, caring for their children and paying visits to their close neighbors. The patriarchal family structure which is dominating the majority of the poor and inhibiting women's work, and the lower rates of female employment are thought to be the main causes of this result.

Öztürk and Çetin (2009) also mentioned unemployment among the causes of poverty. Unemployment is an essential factor of distribution income. The unemployed comprise the main portion of the poor class because they do not participate in the production process and are deprived of revenue sources (Çalışkan, 2010), and child labor is inevitable where poverty exists. Household unemployment is one of the reasons for child labor along with poverty and migration (Karaman and Özçalık, 2007).

Low income is the main criteria of absolute poverty. Considering the average family earnings, it is seen that 25,7% of monthly total family income is below 400 TL and 25,7% is between 400 TL to 800 TL. Participating families who have 2.000 TL or more monthly income comprises the 1% of the sample. According to World Bank's definition, people who earn under 1 or 1,25 USD daily are described to be in absolute poverty. Calculating the minimum absolute poverty limit of an average family of four members, a total income of 435 TL reflects that the family is in absolute poverty, in which case 27,5% of our sample can be classified as absolutely poor. Although there is not a specified standard for the definition of relative poverty, those families measuring up the criteria of Social Assistance and Solidarity Foundation can be interpreted as relatively poor. According to the 2015 data of the Confederation of Turkish Trade Unions, the minimum hunger limit of a family of four is 1.361 TL, and the minimum poverty limit is 4.434 TL (CTTU, 2016). Taking into account these statistics, the vast majority of participants of the research live below the hunger limit, while all continue their lives under the poverty limit. However, the socialization mechanisms should also be mentioned along with these facts. Foundations like the Ministry of Family and Social Policies, municipalities and the Turkish Red Crescent provide allowances both by offering monetary aids and by delivering supplies. Unemployed families' income is mostly provided by these organizations as monetary aids. Aid supplies is particularly provided by municipalities and the Turkish Red Crescent. Aid in the form of food packages, bread and clothing supplies are also common. Thence, although they continue their lives with obvious absolute poverty in monetary terms, not all families are thought to have or reflect an overall absolute poverty due to aid supplies.

In the research, 26,8% of the participators said that they use their income for debt payments, 22,5% said that they use it for dining and kitchen expenses. It can be assumed consistent with the financial situations of the participators of this study. It may seem natural to see participators spend most of their income for debt payment, since the majority of debt is to the banks; bank loan payments may not be easily deferred and deferred payments should involve higher interest rates or result in legal procedures. When the number of the household exceeds four, food and other home expenditures will inevitably rise. In Kaya's 2008 qualitative research, participators who received the Conditional Cash Transfer (CCT) aid - which is granted to raise the school attendance rate of children- stated "We owe to the market, for instance, and as soon as the aid is in our accounts, first thing we do is to pay to the market".

The overall social aid policy in Turkey is predominantly focused on food and health services. In this research, it is also found that the majority of aid people were provided with was food aid first, and health care aid following it.

The participators of the research stated that their meat consumption was limited. The next least consumed food group was fruit and vegetables. Families said that they had more access to dairy products.

The most significant effect of poverty on children is malnutrition. In children who suffer from malnutrition, iodine, ferrum, zinc mineral and vitamin-A deficiency may be observed as well as energy and protein deficiency. Ferrum deficiency is particularly a serious problem for both being much more prevalent and causing irreparable damages (Hatun, 2002). In our research, 27,5% of the participators reported that their children had illnesses due to malnutrition. Almost all mothers who were included in the qualitative study reported that they thought their children were not sufficiently nourished and more than half of the families thought that their children suffered health problems due to malnutrition. Malnutrition rate in childhood in Turkey is 12,3% (UNDP, 2015). Taking families' nourishment data into account, it can be easily concluded that children do not receive the calories sufficiently and evenly. Of the families who participated in the research, 22,8% of them had two or less meals per day. The most serious reflection of malnutrition is on children (Ceren, 2003). Lack of both daily meal numbers and weekly nutrition diversity can be blamed for causing health problems in connection with nutrition such as anemia.

The more the poverty is serious for the household, the less the share of food a family have to distribute, and this fact has more serious results for mothers and their children (Hatun, 2002). Malnutrition threatens 10,9 million children's lives on earth every year and nearly half of these children die every year due to malnutrition (Ceren, 2013). The long term result of malnutrition as an effect of poverty is growth failure in terms of body length. 16,2% of 5-year-old children in Turkey are shorter than their peers. There is a strong correlation between chronic malnutrition and poverty in Turkey (Hatun, 2002). Early childhood diseases and malnutrition also negatively effects a child's learning abilities and thus earning his/her living (UNICEF, 2014).

In context of the research, home environments of the participators were also questioned. The majority of the participating group lived in small apartments with two rooms where kitchen and the living room are together, receiving a decent amount of money as a rent subsidy. Almost half of the participators owned their homes, while 46,6% of the houses were rentals. Nearly half of the tenants said they were paying 0–200 TL for their rental, and others said the monthly rent they paid was over that amount.

Furniture that could cover even basic home requirements including refrigerators and televisions were not owned by some families. ¼ of the families did not have a PC, a tablet, or a dish washer. The majority of the families of three or more persons lived in 50-square meter, 2-room houses. People who participated the research often complained about insufficient number of rooms, poor heating and security problems. In Kocatepe's study (2011) 0,5% of the participators were reported not to have a TV, almost half were living in apartments and 17,3% had a 2-room house. In Ceren's study (2013) it was revealed that 45,4% of the participators lived in 2-room houses, 6,6% did not have a refrigerator and 10,9% did not have a TV. Ceren added that most furniture at the houses were in fact unserviceable. Taş's study (2012) revealed that 21% of the participators sensed themselves poor in respect of housing.

Ocak (2002) generally illustrated the homes of the poor as insufficient in the number of rooms, overcrowded and concluded that the housing facts reflected negative health and environment conditions particularly for children as well as for adults.

From a different point of view, the majority of the families of three or more persons living altogether in 2-room houses may possibly cause damage on the sense of privacy. Assuming that the privacy areas are of vital importance both for parents and adolescents, such housing conditions might mean that either people sacrifice their privacies or children, parents or adolescents interfere with other family members' privacy zones although involuntarily. In developmental terms, this might result in unintended negative results for a child's socio-emotional and sexual development. The inadequacy of space might even inhibit the motor development. Having to do homework in a crowded house without a private room might sabotage school performance, causing academic failure. Children living in crowded and inappropriate home environments will not exhibit the desired educational success or performance (UNICEF, 2005).

All participators who were finally asked what poverty meant to them defined poverty with terms such as; barehandedness, state of dependency, difficulty, desperation, unhappiness and despair. When asked about their worries of their children's future they mentioned topics including education, occupation, earning a living and money resources, security, bad habits, improper environment or friendships, health, death of parents, crime and marriage.

As mentioned above, the sense of desperation, continuous high level distress, worries about the future which were caused by poverty harms individuals' physical and mental health; the prevalence of medical conditions related to distress like hypertension or asthma and psychosocial problems like depression, dismay, problematic relations or substance addiction might rise. Distress sources emerging parallel to poverty might affect parents' abilities of providing their children with sensitive and tender care, which maximizes the brain development and has a lifetime effect on the child (Zuckerman and Sandel, 2013). Regarding this fact, depression symptoms of the participators were observed and it was revealed that only 18% of the participators told that they had not been distressed for the past week. More than half of the participators reflected lack of interest, while ¾ reported that they had been in distress for the past two years.

Within the research context participators were asked child oriented questions such as number of children they had, children's ages, educational status, health, playing, occupational status or needs. From this part of the discussion, findings conducted from the participators' answers about their children are commented in connection with the literature.

Most participators had two children, the majority of whom attended primary school. Children were mostly found to continue their education at classes consistent to their ages, whereas 20% were at lower classes according to their ages. Although at school age, the number of children who do not attend to school throughout the world is 121 million. Poverty is an obstacle for children to benefit from the right of education, because the poor families cannot afford school expenses, governments cannot provide sufficient amount of funds for education or for the worst part, child labor becomes more prominent to supplement the household income. In the developing countries 13% of 7–18 age children has never attended an educational facility, which means a total of 140 million. Over 300 million children in the developing countries continue their lives without informational tools or media such as television, radio, newspapers and telephone (UNICEF, 2005).

In this research, it was revealed that the majority of the children attended primary school at the appropriate age. Only 9,8% of the children received preschool education. According to UNICEF's 2003–2005 data on child poverty in Turkey, the rate of preschool attendance between 3–6 years was 16% (UNICEF, 2016). The more recent statistics of Ministry of National Education as of 2011–2012, indicates that the rate of preschool attendance of children between 3–5 years, between 4–5 years and over five years was 30,87%, 44,04% and 65,69%, respectively (MINISTRY OF FAMILY AND SOCIAL POLICY, 2016). The lower schooling rate of our sample is noteworthy and indicates that particular effort must be made to support preschool education. 2003 Nobel Economy Award winner James Heckman's studies showed that the return on investment (ROI) rate of education is higher if development is supported at early ages, a minimum return of USD 7 for a dollar spent at early childhood (Heckman, 2012).

In our study, the majority of children were found to be at the compulsory schooling age and to continue their education. Of those who did not pursue their education, the majority quit after secondary school. The Ministry of National Education's statistics of 2011–2012, which indicates that the schooling rate of children in primary and secondary school was 98,67% and 67,37% respectively, can be commented on to support our study's findings (MINISTRY OF FAMILY AND SOCIAL POLICY, 2013). Families who were interviewed in this study described their children's reasons of quitting education as children's refusal of attending school, financial problems and child labor. According to data collected in the qualitative analysis level of the study, the rate of families who cannot provide educational resources to their children is 40%. This rate is comparatively higher in respect of the quantitative data and inconsistent with information given by the families. Parents were asked whether their children pursued education regularly, and while most responses were positive, it was found that a minority continued education unsteadily. A downfall in the rate of attendance to school might be observed lately due to the recent change of compulsory schooling age (60 months), the separation of primary education into two phases, late schooling, unpreparedness to school and/or experiencing difficulties in transition to 5th class from the 4th. Significant inequalities are seen in secondary school attendance between regions, urban-rural settlements, socio-economic conditions and genders. Discontinuity of school attendance is also another phenomenon as a result of child labor or housework, or reluctance to education (UNICEF, 2012). Parallel annotations of families show the deepness of the problem.

As the findings of the study reveal, while almost all families desired their children to attend a school, only ¼ of the families wanted their children to work. Every three families of the four who wanted their children to work told that they needed more money, the remaining citing that they were trying to have their children learn a craft to earn their living. Children who are exposed to environmental risk factors and who are deprived of tender care and stimuli, certainly a frequent phenomenon common in poor families, will probably have to face health disturbing and safety threatening working conditions throughout their lives for the sake of supporting their families, if they do not receive the required education for their optimal development in the following ages. The earlier a child economically begins to support his/her family, the more he/she is continuously engaged in the work life for his contribution to the family budget. Children who begin work life as early as small ages in harsh working conditions where their health and safety is endangered for very low wages when compared to their labor, also suffer from difficulties in continuing their education. It has been reported that millions of children all over the world are forced to join the workforce to contribute to their household income, which interrupts their education, hinders them living their childhood, strikes their optimal physical and mental development (Durgun, 2011; UNICEF, 2014). Child labor, common in Turkey, has reflections in our study's findings too. Among the reasons of the increase of child labor are parents' insensitivity, inadequacy of legal arrangements, along with families' perception that their child will be a grown up only by working and standing on his/her own feet, and the belief that this would contribute to the child's education.

It was found from the research that the majority of the children had social security, the most having a Green Card, the following most frequent security sources being benefits of Social Security Institution, Social Security Organization for Artisans and the Self-Employed and State Pension Fund, respectively. 24 children were found not to have any social security. Only one third of the mothers were found to receive health care at the suggested frequency during pregnancy. The participators were found to stick to the schedules for health monitoring and vaccination more carefully and responsibly for their babies compared to mothers at pregnancy, although under the ideally desired level. It was revealed that 3,7% of the babies had never been taken to a routine health control. Most participators told that they had gone to a healthcare center for consultation only when their child suffered an illness, while 5,6% stated that they had never applied to any healthcare facility.

Main healthcare indicators of children's well-being include vaccination rates, availability of healthcare services, having social security, accessibility of healthcare services both during pregnancy and afterbirth, and child mortality prevalence. Vaccination has a vital importance for the protection of baby health, vaccination statistics being a fundamental indicator for health monitoring. According to 2008 Turkey Demographic and Health Survey results on vaccination data, the rate of fully vaccinated children was 45,7% as of 1998, and it reached 80,5% by the end of 2008. 1,6% of the children did not have any kind of vaccination as of 2008. However, there is not a centrally gathered comprehensive information system in which child statistics are collected on age, gender, socio-economical condition, etc., and by which well-being indicators were kept. Particularly in national reports on child rights, considerable coordination problems are experienced in collating various data from all the foundations which serve children. In monitoring nationwide services, complaints panels, declaration, information and consulting mechanisms should be developed (MINISTRY OF FAMILY AND SOCIAL POLICY, 2013).

In the study it was revealed that 88,2% of the children did not have any serious health problems, while 10,5% do. 7% of the children had an untreated health problem and 13,5% had special needs due to developmental disabilities. It is presumed that 17%–20% of the children have chronic diseases, a rate that can be considered even higher when less serious health conditions are taken into account (Schonfeld and Perrin, 2013). In a USA study on the course of the frequency of developmental disabilities at childhood over years, it was revealed that one in six children (16,7%) was found to have a developmental disability between 2006 and 2008, and that this rate has been increasing for the past 10 years (Boyle et al., 2011). Parallel to WHO's estimations and as defined in Turkey Disability Survey, people with special needs account for at least 10% of Turkey's total population (Ertem et al., 2012). These surveys being not sufficiently comprehensive in respect of childhood, it might be presumed that children with special needs account for not below 10%–16% of the public, rates that are parallel to the findings of our research.

In the study, 27,5% of the families who asserted that their children had health problems, also added that the health problem their child experienced was related with malnutrition. To another question about malnutrition of their children, 82% of the families responded that their children were not nourished healthily, while 16,7% thought their children had adequate and healthful nourishment. The majority of the children had two or three meals per day, while 1,5% had only one daily meal. Poverty plays the main role in malnutrition for children by causing inadequacy of food obtained for the household, bringing about home stress and chronic fatigue for mothers and thus causing breastmilk discontinue earlier, causing pregnant mothers' malnutrition and thus babies' low birth weight, conducing unhealthy physical environment and inadequate healthcare services. Poverty, at the same time, deepens the problem of malnutrition by mothers' illiteracy. According to the analysis in 2002 WHO Health Report, it was pointed out that low birth weight arouses as a big problem in all regions where poverty spreads. WHO presumes that 27% of the children throughout the world have lower weights than they should have in comparison with their peers, and that the majority of these children live in the developing countries (Hatun, 2002).

16% of the children under five years old experience malnutrition by inadequate and unhealthy food in the developing countries. These children face the risks of anemia, anergy and ill health (UNICEF, 2005). According to the data from UNICEF's study on poverty in Turkey between 2003–2005, food poverty regressed to 20,5% as of 2005 from 28,1% of 2003 (UNICEF, 2016). In summary, in developing countries, one in three children is exposed to shelter deprivation, one in five fresh water and one in seven basic healthcare (UNICEF, 2005).

In the study, almost all participators use the domestic water system for drinking water, only a minority have to use the plumbing system outside of their houses. According to UNICEF, among child poverty indicators are baby and child mortality rates, lower weighted and shorter child rates under five years compared to desired limits, the rate of population that can access fresh water, the rate of accessibility of sufficient hygiene and healthcare, the rate of children's fully vaccination and finally, the rate of children that begin their education at primary school level (BIANET, 2016). Accessibility of fresh water is one of the most important poverty criteria accepted all over the world. Nearly 400 million children worldwide suffer a lack of fresh water. In developing countries, one in three children are deprived of fresh water (UNICEF, 2005). Considering that four in five children have to walk at least 15 minutes to access a fresh water reservoir in deserts of southern Africa, people qualified as comparatively poor in Turkey cannot be classified as poor in this respect. Though assumed to live in poverty from other aspects, the foundations maintaining municipality and utilities services in Turkey can be considered to have fulfilled their responsibilities in providing fresh water.

Among the questions directed to families is whether school expenses and requirements are fulfilled and how. 48,5% of the families said that they cannot afford educational expenses, while 42,4% said they can, the majority reporting that they spent 1 to 100 TL or over 500 TL. 43,9% said that they spent 1 to 100 TL for school expenses; items of expenditure ranking from high to low are notebooks, books, stationery, pocket money for students, school fees, clothing and school shuttles.

62,5% of the families reported that they received financial aid from someone else for school expenses, while 27% told they did not. The resources of aid are Social Assistance and Solidarity Foundation (42,2%), the school administration (15%), close family and relatives (9,7%), other foundations, guilds and municipalities. By the Low No. 3294 of Conditional Cash Transfer (CCT), financial support aid is granted by Social Assistance and Solidarity Foundation to mothers who have children between seven to 18 years old that continue their education at primary, secondary and high schools, provided that they do not quit their education (CCT Guide, 2016). Some families stated that they continue their living with the help of this aid. Socio-Economical Aid is also provided by the Ministry of Family and Social Policies to eligible families that are dependent on 3rd party support. Municipalities and some private sector companies also help families with educational expenses in cash or by delivering supplies.

Families were asked what other expenses they have for their children other than education. 49,3% of the families said that they could give their children pocket money, ranging daily from 0–1 TL to 2–3 TL. Thought provoking and noteworthy is that unmet needs of children include clothing, PC, telephone, toys, educational materials and stationery and even medication. 5% of the children said that they wanted to go on vacation but they could not. Information has been attained that, having not fulfilled this need, the children showed affliction, huff, comparison with peers and blame his/her own family for the deprivation, while only a minority showed that they understood their families' conditions.

From the perspective of not accessing the requirements they desired to reach, the children qualify as "relatively poor" when compared with the remaining public. Though they desire to have, the children said that they cannot access electronical devices, clothing, some courses or musical instruments. Those children who cannot have these materials expressed high levels of affliction. However, more than half of the children in this condition stated that they have never had any argument with their families. This helps paraphrasing the situation of these children as "learned helplessness". The majority of the children said that they would share their pocket money with their friends. Of the children of the families who participated in the study, the reason of the presence of high level of sharing can be described as socially disadvantaged and pro-socially active children's having higher level of empathy than their peers. The soul should be nourished for being not demolished by poverty, and this requires the involvement of sharing, tenderness and conscience in individuals' lives (Hatun, 2012). By sharing and being in one another's shoes, children might be assumed to try to reduce the social and psychological effects of poverty on themselves. In the qualitative study, the rate of 20% of one of the answers of the children "I would have helped others!" to the question "What would you do, should you have a magic wand in your hand?" reflects this finding.

In the study, it was found that the majority of the children did not work, only nine of them (2,2%) did, three working at a mechanic shop, three at a cafe or restaurant, one at a market/open bazaar and two at different jobs. Seven of these children were 16–19 years old, one was 12–15 years old, one was 4–7 years old. Four worked for more than 12 hours, three worked for 8–11 hours, one for 4–7 hours and one for 0–3 hours, daily. Weekly working hours was 36 for seven of them and 16–25 hours for two. Seven of the children went to work every day since they do not continue their education, one worked on weekends and one after school hours. Of the working children seven used their wages for household expenses, while the other two children's earnings were used mainly for their school expenses. Eight said that they loved the job they were doing. One child said that he did not like his job, explaining that he was working at a mechanic shop where his senior fellows and other craftsman were not treating him good. Eight of the children told that they did not have any fears or feel bad while working, while one expressed the opposite.

TurkStat's 2012 data showed that 5,9% (893.000) of 12.247.000 6–17-year-old children were part of the workforce. Of these working children 68,75% (614.000) are boys and 31,25% (279.000) are girls. Of the mentioned child labor force 49,83% were also attending school, while the remaining 50,17% did not continue their education. As for the age groups, of these working children 81,8% of the 6–14 years old and 34,3% of the 15–17 years old continued their education. Given that compulsory schooling is regulated for 6–14-year-old children by the government authority and child labor is prohibited for this age span, according to these statistics, of the 292.000 children of this age group approximately 20% has abandoned compulsory education, and 66% of the 15–17-year-old age children did not continue secondary education (MINISTRY OF FAMILY AND SOCIAL POLICY, 2013). Parallel to the findings of this research, schooling ends for the majority of the children who enter the work force early, their socialization process evolves and continues with working conditions along with risks ranging from malnutrition, various types of accidents, tendency of violence, life in streets to getting involved in crimes. Aside from the prohibition of employing 6–14 year olds by law, the employment of children who are the participators of our research at as early as 4–7 years, or with more direct words, "forcing 4 to 7 year olds to work" reflects the seriousness of the problem.

Participators reported that few children had friends who worked or lived in the streets, and that few children had bad habits. These bad habits include smoking, lying, alcohol use, running away from home, theft and glue-sniffing or huffing. Most children were not involved in any crime. Of those 14 children who were accused to have been involved in crime, 10 were convicted.

In the research, it was found that the majority of the children lived at their home, though 21 (5,1%) were rough-sleeping and were not going to their families' homes. Four children did not come home for a few days without informing their families and one child left for a couple of weeks without notice. 12 participators left our questions on leaving home without permission or on rough-sleeping unanswered. Child and adolescent support centers continue special projects on the prevention of home leaving by facilitating housing, education and rehabilitation, aiming to win back children to public, a service that should be made more efficient with the collaboration of related fields (MINISTRY OF FAMILY AND SOCIAL POLICY, 2013).

Home environment is, just like for many children, the most important, the most valuable and basic potential environment for children to support their development, who suffer from and persevere many risks caused by poverty. For a child to develop in every field of development, physical conditions of the house, mother-child interaction, stimuli at home and child care is of great importance along with his/her physical health (Hatun, 2002).

In the research, it was found that the majority of the children did not have a separate room. Additionally, the rate of children's not having a personal toy was comparatively high (60%). In the USA, a study on the risk factors of home environments of the children living in poverty areas revealed that, food and diaper needs of 11% of the children were not met, 16% of the children lived in rooms not bright enough to see another person's facial expressions, 22% of the children had to have their meals on their own without any manipulation, 27% were continuously taken care of by other children where no adult was present (Ertem et al., 1997). The data collected in the qualitative measurement of this study showed that one of the first things children would have changed should they were reborn would be their home environment, reflecting the discontent of the children of their homes.

From the perspective of parent-child interactions, participators were asked how they reacted to their children's wrong actions. Half of the participators replied that they would get angry and shout, some told that they talked with their children on the fault he/she had made, a portion confessed that they had beaten their children as punishment and a minority said that they would ignore the wrong behavior. 73% of the parents spent time to play with their children, while 20% told that they could not.

On the stimuli in the home environment, the time spent by the children in front of the TV was questioned. Findings showed that 42,6% of the children spent 1–2 hours, 38,2% spent 3–4 hours and 6,2% spent five or more hours watching TV per day. According to Radio and Television Supreme Council's 2006 "Television Watching Habits of Primary School Children" research, 82% of the children in Turkey determined how long they would spend time watching television and which shows to watch. 28,4% of the participating students of our study watch TV for five or more hours, 20,8% watch TV for two hours and 18,1% watch TV for three hours on daily basis. The time spent before TV by the students on weekends is more than 2,5-3 times of the work days. According to this data, having calculated that a student spends 900 hours at school and 1.500 hours before TV at total every year, it can easily be concluded that TV fills a significant space in children's daily lives (MINISTRY OF FAMILY AND SOCIAL POLICY, 2013).

Caused by poverty, the deprivation of printed media, PC, the internet, video games and mobile phones, which in usual circumstances can by itself be harmful when used long term and inappropriately, increases the intensity of TV addiction. TV commercials captivate children more than any other show because they are much shorter and more vivid, and children tend to watch commercials from beginning to the end for a very long time without blinking an eye. Thus the child's brain which is still in the development process is filled with the desire of consumption of brand marks (PCG, 2012). Our research findings also include families' experienced difficulties in meeting the children's desires. Consequently, TV not only leaves children in destitute of stimuli and makes them observe wrong role models or facts that they cannot comprehend, but also increases unmet desires of consumption, influencing child - family communication and interaction negatively. Children should be safeguarded from these electronical, digital and virtual menaces.

Besides the wish to change their home environment if they had a magic wand, the other three things children expressed that they would have changed were their educational situation, health conditions and their parents' status. It can be commented that a child expresses his/her opinion about the most individually distinct subject or area where he/she lives and feels poverty more drastically. Terms of relative poverty such as shelter poverty, health poverty or educational poverty substantiate the children's answers. Answers of wishes about the public issues such as wars and terror to end, people to be more gracious, testify that these children are more sensitive on empathy.

In qualitative findings of the research children were asked to define poverty. In this context, while the majority defined poverty as "not fulfilling the needs", 41,1% said that poverty is an "economical difficulty". Öztürk (2009) defines poverty as the condition of earning under a certain amount of income, or - in general terms- the deprivation of economic, social and cultural rights and failing to earn the sufficient amount of income. It is considered that children's poverty descriptions vary on how they live it. Poverty cannot solely be defined with the terms of economical context, but deprivation of social and health needs should also be taken into consideration. With this approach emerged the term "relative poverty". This fact has strong correlation with children's answers about the definition of poverty such as "unemployment", "being driven into crime" and "psychological problems". The participating children can be said not only to live poverty in a financial context, but they also directly sense relative poverty. When asked about their personal choices of occupation, they generally mentioned jobs which they easily encounter in the environment and professions from which they can absorb positive models, such as teacher or police officer, professions which their families' working conditions will probably direct them to be one of them someday. Another reason for these profession choices might be presumed that the majority of the family members do not have such occupations and these professions are considered as having probably higher social status than their family members' jobs.

The sample of the research consists of parents who applied to Mamak District Social Assistance and Solidarity Foundation and of those who earned social aid. The most significant restraint of this study is that it has been conducted on a basis of only one township district, which is planned to be extended with further research. But this study successfully reached a multidimensional and comprehensive structure throughout the process with a workshop at the final stage, along with quantitative and qualitative data analysis. The workshop laid the groundwork for sharing and contribution of the research findings with countless experts from the field and with authorized people of the district, heading towards an action plan concentrated particularly on resolutions.

5. Conclusions and Recommendations

In this study, the poverty status of the families which are registered in Mamak District Social Assistance and Solidarity Foundation that adheres to province of Ankara Mamak District was examined. The research findings; the majority of parents compared to 82.6% mothers composed, 16.9% was composed of father. That most of the parents are woman due to interviews conducted during daytime, father of the position of head of the family were outside the household to meet their household needs or it stems from fathers guidance to the mothers to answer questions.

In this study, interview forms with closed-ended and open-ended questions which contain age, gender, job, educational status, marital status, socio-demographic characteristics; educational status age and health and nutritional status of children as well as emigration status, physical conditions that families have, working conditions and debt, their views on poverty were applied to families which are supported from the Mamak District Social Assistance and Solidarity Foundation.

Parents who participated in the interviews, defined poverty mainly as, can not meet their needs, unemployment; in parallel it seemed that children defined poverty, can not meet their needs and economic difficulties.

At most of the families which participated to the interviews, it has been shown that parents have low education level. Although families have low educational level, they want that their children to receive a good education and have a good job. Accordingly, the ratio of children to continue education is high. The vast majority of children started elementary school on time and the vast majority of children continued education and training at age of compulsory education. Almost half of the parents stated that they have difficulties in financing training costs and the majority of the families stated that they could spend up 100 Turkish Lira for their children's education per month. At the same time, it is observed that most of the families receive support to meet the educational needs of their children. But half of the parents reported that their children experienced disruptions in continuing education because of poverty.

When family type is examined, it was found that the nuclear family are widespread. When the children data are examined, families have two children or three children, families stated that children are malnourished, a large part of children do not have pre-school education (83,1%), most of the parents can not meet their children's educational expenses, but they receive support for educational expenses.

Considering marital status of parents, although the vast majority of the participants are officially married (74,5%), one in four are divorced or their spouse has passed away. Divorced parents stated their grounds for divorce are mainly violence, financial difficulties or bad habits. The vast majority of divorced parents (90,5%) stated that they do not get alimony. Also the vast majority of divorced or widow parents (94,6%) stated that they do not receive an orphan's pension.

In terms of health insurance, most families get support from social assistance and solidarity foundation, they also get medical assistance from the state. Nevertheless families without health insurance were seen. Some of the families who were interviewed stated they could not take the drugs because of the expense.

It has been observed that parents health problems but it was seen that the majority do not treated with drugs and also drugs which used from the majority of treated drug are covered by the state. It was also seen that the disabled people in families, 67 (16,4%) and two in three people with disabilities receive support from the state. It was determined that the majority of the families take their sick children to the health center, have regular vaccines, and consequently the vast majority of children do not have a significant disease.

When the families' consumption patterns are analyzed, it was observed that almost all of families hardly ever consume meat and meat products; they consume vegetables and fruits once in a month, and milk and milk products several times a week. A majority of parents stated that malnourished children, one in four children (27,5%) have health problems that are malnutrition-related.

When examining the type of assistance, It was determined that they receive assistance from especially Mamak District Social Assistance and Solidarity Foundation, Ankara Metropolitan Municipality, Ministry of Family And Social Policy, relatives and neighbors.

When working conditions are examined, it was observed that, almost all women are housewives, are not gainfully employed, the small number of female employees usually work in everyday tasks such as cleaning jobs. The men are generally unemployed or have been working in non-permanent and temporary jobs like peddle, construction worker, paper gathering. It was seen that only a few of children (9) have a job.

One-third of the families included in the interviews (33%) came to Ankara with immigration. Most of the migrants came from different cities, towns and villages. Health problems, job opportunities, their children's education and marriage are among the causes of migration.

When residential housing types are examined, while the vast majority are in an apartment (1+1), some are in a slum. General problems of the house are moisture, cold, security issues, and house is small. Many families lives in Public Housing Authority (TOKI) houses that families pay low payment rates and have the opportunity to become homeowners.

Analyzing the places where food shopping, bazaar and the market comes first, it is among the peddlers and grocery store the answers are given too. Some families have stated that they collect food waste and garbage from the bazaars.

When meeting the clothing needs of the family situation is examined, it was determined that they are trying to meet the needs from the market, the peddlers, used and second hand relative / clothes of their neighbors for help, but the vast majority of parents indicated that they can not meet the needs of children's clothes. This situation leads to arguments with the children and their family and families are sad and unhappy.

When the interviewees debt situation is analyzed, the vast majority were found to be in debt. The amount of debt was found to be much greater than 5000 Turkish Lira; almost half of the borrowers were found to be in debt to the bank.

When the family situation of giving money to the children is examined, it was shown that more than half of children think that their allowance is not enough. Most of the children stated that they bought food at school with their pocket money.

According to the testimony of children who participated in the interviews, although they want an object, they could get it – these objects included; computers, cell phones, clothing, toys. To the parallel of children's response, the objects which their children want but they can not buy are computers, mobile phones, clothes, toys and food. When children's need can not be met, they usually are unhappy and sad, their mothers feel sadness, despair and unhappy too.

Most of the children prefer a job like the police and soldiers when they grow up. It is contemplated that this situation is due to that children are faced with the police and the gendarmerie because of security events in their local area.

Parents stated that what they want to change about themselves are have good work, good education status, a happy marriage and a more prosperous life. Nonetheless it is identified that they want the end of terrorism and war, reduced poverty and the provision of social cohesion and solidarity. The children want to change where they live, poverty status, and getting a better education. Also it was seen that children want people to treat each other better, the end of terrorism and war and that everyone is equal.

A workshop was conducted with the participation of various public institutions and organizations in the field of child poverty in this study, and civil society organizations working in the authorities. In the workshop, group sessions were conducted about child poverty and the prevention of child poverty. There are lots of experts who work in the Mamak district that attended the workshop and within the workshop an action plan was prepared, short and long term goals determined, and suggested responsible institutions to carry out the actions.

The following suggestions can be made about poverty;

- For poverty reduction in Ankara and other provinces, the short and long term strategies and policies should be determined about this issue.
- Social policies should be developed to reduce unemployment and to correct social inequalities.
- Parents should be supported through training to prevent child poverty.
- All educational expenses of the children should be covered by the state until the end of university.
- Planning and implementation of micro, meso and macro-scale policies and poverty alleviation programs are essential.
- Considering the ecological systems theory, necessary arrangements should be made in combating poverty.

- The fight against poverty must be addressed not only at the local level but also necessary measures should be taken at the international level.
- Health systems must be strengthened, it should also be provided that drugs should be free to all citizens.
- Additional job opportunities should be provided for unemployed people.
- Social assistance applicants should be evaluated as soon as possible and answers should be given to the owners.
- To provide developmental screening and early intervention services, child development specialists should be increased in order to prevent growth retardation that can occur in children.
- Pre-school education should be encouraged for children of families with a low socio-economic level.
- Promotion of vocational training courses should be made for unemployed parents.
- Daycare centers and kindergartens must be provided in areas with low socio-economic status to support the work of parents.
- Food distribution should be carried out in all schools to avoid poor diet-induced diseases, developmental delays and disabilities.
- Collection fees like examination paper reproduction, supplementary books, and test books must be prevented from children attending school.
- Children whose families have a low socio-economic status should undergo health checks that should be provided at least twice a year.
- Public transport should be free for children at schools' entry and exit times.
- Parents are concerned about losing social assistance and work illegally therefore losing social assistance rules according to working legally needs to evaluated and revised.
- Parents who have working facilities can be placed in suitable jobs and salaries can be paid according to their social assistance. In this way the abuse of social benefits can be avoided and more needy families benefit from social assistance.
- It can be suggested to prepare and implement action plans related to poverty.

6. References

Aktaş, G. (2013). Yoksulluğu ev içinden tanımlamak: kadın bakış açısından yoksulluk. vıı. Ulusal Sosyoloji Kongresi (ed. M. Tuna). Erişim tarihi: 28 Mart 2016, http://sosyolojikongresi.org/ekitap/cilt%201pdf≠page=28.

ASAGEM.(2010). Sosyal yardım algısı ve yoksulluk kültürü. Erişim tarihi: 25 Mart 2016, http://ailetoplum.aile.gov.tr/data/54293ea2369 dc32358ee2b25/kutuphane_59_sosyal_yardim_algisi_ve_yoksulluk_ kulturu.pdf.

ASPB (Aile ve Sosyal Politikalar Bakanlığı) (2013). Ulusal Çocuk Hakları Strateji Belgesi ve Eylem Planı. Erişim Tarihi: 30 Nisan 2016. http:// cocukhizmetleri.aile.gov.tr/data/54ad4cd6369dc5dac028bda2/ulusal_ cocuk_haklari_strateji_belgesi_ve_eylem_plani.pdf.

Aung, S. M. (2015). Responding to child abuse in myanmar: poverty, ethnicity and religion in pathein. *The Review of Faith & International Affairs, 13 (4)*, 79–81.

Bakırtaş, T. ve Kardemir, O. (2012). Türkiye'de yetersiz eğitim ve yoksulluk ilişkisi: iller bazında ekonometrik bir analiz. Erişim tarihi: 07 Mart 2016, https://www.researchgate.net/publication/281641627.

BIANET (2016). Yoksulluk ve çocuklar üzerine etkileri. Erişim Tarihi: 01 Mart 2016, http://bianet.org/bianet/cocuk/35699-yoksulluk-etkileri

BIANET.(2016). Çocuk yoksulluğu, artıyor, bütçelerde artmalı. Erişim Tarihi: 02 Mart 2016, http://bianet.org/bianet/80212-cocuk-yoksullugu-artiyor-butceler-de-artmali.

Bilgin, R. (2009). Diyarbakır'da sokakta çalışan çocuklar üzerine sosyolojik bir araştırma. *Elektronik Sosyal Bilimler Dergisi, 8 (27)*, 232–244.

Boyle, C. A., Boulet, S., Schieve, L. A., Cohen, R. A., Blumberg, S. J., Yeargin-Allsopp, M., Visser, S., Kogan, M. D. (2011). Trends in the prevalence of developmental disabilities in us children, 1997–2008. *Pediatrics, 127(6)*, 1034–42.

Ceren, A. (2013). Kentsel yoksullukla mücadelede kamu kurumları ve sivil toplum kuruluşları rolü: Adıyaman kent yoksulları üzerine bir alan araştırması. Yüksek Lisans Tezi, Gazi Üniversitesi, Ankara.

Datta, S. K. ve Singh, K.(2015). Analysis of child deprivation ın ındia: focus on health and educational perspectives. Economic analysis and policy. Erişim tarihi: 28 Mart 2016. http://dxdo:org/101016/jeap2016.03.003.

Dickerson, A. ve Popli, G. K. (2015). Persistent poverty and children's cognitive development: Evidence from The UK Millenium Cohort Study. *Journal of The Royal Statistical Society, 179 (2), 535–558.*

Dornan, P. ve Pells, K. (2015). Building strong foundations for later livelihoods by addressing child poverty: evidence from younglives. *Enterprise Development and Microfinance, 26 (2),* 90–103.

Durgun, Ö.(2011). Türkiye'de yoksulluk ve çocuk yoksulluğu üzerine bir inceleme. *The Journal of Knowledge Economy & Knowledge Management, 6(1),* 143–154.

Erkan, B., Bağlı, M. (2005). Göç ve yoksulluk alanında kentle bütünleşme eğilimi: Diyarbakır örneği. *Hacettepe Üniversitesi Edebiyat Fakültesi Dergisi Cilt, 22 (1),* 105–124.

Ertem, İ. Ö., Çakmak, N. M., Ünal, C., Gök, C. G. (2012). Çocuklar için özel gereksinim raporuna geçiş: özürlülük ölçütü, sınıflandırması ve özürlülere verilecek sağlık kurulu raporları hakkında yönetmeliğin bilimsel incelemesi. Ankara: UNICEF Türkiye Ülke Ofisi.

Eryurt, M. A. ve Koç, İ. (2009). Yoksulluk ve çocuk ölümlülüğü: Hane halkı refah düzeyinin çocuk ölümlülüğü üzerindeki etkisi. *Çocuk Sağlığı ve Hastalıkları Dergisi, 52,* 113–121.

Frieberg. D., Lundkvist, K. Xinjun, L. ve Sundquist, K. (2015). Parental poverty and occupation as risk factors for pediatric sleep disordered breathing. *Sleep Medicine, 16 (2015),* 1169–1175.

Gün, Z., Bayraktar, F. (2008). Türkiye'de iç göçün ergenlerin uyumundaki rolü. *Türk Psikiyatri Dergisi.*

Hanson, J. L., Hair, N., Shan, D. G., Shi, F., Gilmore, J. H.,Wolfe, B. L. ve Pollak, D. S. (2013). Family poverty affects the rate of human ınfant brain growth. *PLOS ONE, 8 (12),* 1–9.

Hatun, S (2002). Çocuk hakları sözleşmesinin 13. yılında yoksulluk ve çocuklar üzerine etkileri. Erişim tarihi: 07 Mart 2016, www.ttb.org.tr/eweb/yoksulluk_ve_cocuklar.pdf.

Heckman, J. (2012). Invest in early childhood development: reduce deficits, strengthen the economy. "the heckman equation". *National Institute For Early Childhood Education Research.* Erişim Tarihi: 30 Nisan 2016 file:///C:/Users/user/Downloads/F_HeckmanDeficitPiececeCUSTOM-Generic_052714.pdf.

Karaman, B. ve Özçalık, M. (2007). Türkiye'de gelir dağılımı eşitsizliğinin bir sonucu: Çocuk işgücü. *Yönetim ve Ekonomi,* 14 (1).

Karasar, N. (1999). Bilimsel araştırma yöntemi, Ankara: Nobel Yayınları.

Kaya, İ. (2008). Yoksullukla mücadelede eğitimin rolü: şartlı nakit transferi ŞNT örneği. Yayımlanmamış Yüksek Lisans Tezi, Süleyman Demirel Üniversitesi, Isparta.

Kaya, Z. (2011). Türkiye'de yoksulluk analizi: bir probit model uygulaması. Yayınlanmamış Yüksek Lisans Tezi, Atatürk Üniversitesi, Erzurum.

Kocatepe, H., (2011) Yoksulluk ve Kent Yoksulluğu: Yalova İli Örneği. Yalova Üniversitesi Sosyal Bilimler Enstitüsü Yüksek Lisans Tezi.

Koyun, A. ve Çiçekoğlu, P. (2011). Karanlıkta kaybolan umutlar. *Anadolu Hemşirelik ve Sağlık Bilimleri Dergisi, 14 (1), 59–65.*

Lessard, N. L., Alcala, E. ve Capitman, J. A. (2016). Pollution, poverty and potentially preventable childhood morbidity ın central california. *The Journal of Pediatrics, 168,* 11–13.

Ocak E. (2002) Yoksulun evi, ", Necmi Erdoğan (Editör) Yoksulluk Halleri: Türkiye'de Kent Yoksulluğunun Toplumsal Görüntüleri Demokrasi Kitaplığı Yayınları.

Özmen, E., Özmen, D., Dündar, P. E., Çetinkaya, A. Ç. ve Taşkın, F. O. (2008). Yoksulluğun ergenlerin ruh sağlığına etkileri. Erişim tarihi: 28 Mart 2016, https://wwwresearchgate.net/publication/267511102.

Öztürk, A. B. (2008). Kentteki çocuk yoksulluğu: Keçiören örneği. Yayınlanmamış Yüksek Lisans Tezi, Hacettepe Üniversitesi, Ankara.

Öztürk, M. Ve Çetin, I. (2009). Dünyada ve Türkiye'de yoksulluk ve kadınlar. *Journal of Yasar University, 3 (11),* 2661–2698

PDR (Psikolojik Danışmanlık ve Rehberlik Servisi) (2012). Erişim Tarihi: 30 Nisan 2016 http://berkio.feza.k12.tr/dosyalar/4721191014.pdf

Sameroff, A. J., Seifer, R. Baldwin, A. ve Baldwin, C. (1993). Stability of intelligence from preschool to adolescence: the influence of social and family risk factors. *Child Development, 64 (1),* 80–97.

Santiago, C. D., Kaltman, S. ve Mirando, J. (2013). Poverty and mental health: how do low income adults and children fare in psychotherapy? *Journal of Clinical Psychology, 69 (2),* 115–126.

Schonfeld, D. J. ve Perrin, E. C. (2013). Hastalığa uyum. M. Yurdakök (Çeviri Editörü), *Rudolph pediatri* (ss. 368–370). Ankara: Güneş Tıp Kitabevleri.

Sharam, A. ve Hulse, K. (2015). Understanding then exus between poverty and homelessness: relational poverty analysis of families: experiencing homelessness in Australia Housing. *Theory and Science, 31 (3)*, 294–309.

Şeniz Ertürk, P. (2010) Yoksulluk olgusu. Yüksek Lisans Tezi, Anadolu Üniversitesi, Eskişehir.

ŞNT Rehberi. Erişim Tarihi: 19 Nisan 2006 http://www.sosyalyardimlar. net/sartli-nakit-transferi-rehberi/.

Tampubolon, G. (2016). Growing up in poverty, growing old in ınfirmity the long arm of childhood conditions in great britain. *PLOS ONE, 10 (12)*, 1–16.

Taş, R., (2012) Ankara'nın Kentsel Yoksulluk Haritası. Turgut Özal Üniversitesi Yayınları.

TIS (2016). Erişim tarihi: 07 Mart 2016, http://www.hurriyet.com.tr/4-kisilik-ailenin-aclik-siniri-1-361-+130177740.

UNDP (2004). Erişim tarihi: 26 Mart 2016, http://erc.undp.org/.

UNDP (2014). 2014 İnsani gelişme raporu. Erişim tarihi: 27 Mart 2016, http://www.tr.undp.org/content/turkey/tr/home/library/human_development/hdr-2014.html.

UNDP (2015). Human development report. Erişim tarihi: 03 Mart 2016, http://www.tr.undp.org/content/turkey/tr/home/library/humandevelopment/human-development-report-2015html.

UNICEF (2005). Dünya çocuklarının durumu. Erişim Tarihi: 07 Mart 2016, www.unıcef.org/turkey/pdf/-dcd05.pdf.

UNICEF (2013). United Nations children's fund, committing to child survival: a promise renewed, progress report 2013. Erişim tarihi: 25 Mart 2016, http://www.unicef.org/lac/Committing_to_Child_Survival_APR_9_Sept_2013.pdf.

UNICEF (2014). Sayılarla dünya çocuklarının durumu raporu. Erişim tarihi: 27 Mart 2016, http://www.unicef.org.tr/files/bilgimerkezi/doc/Unicef%20SOWC%202014%20web.pdf.

UNICEF (2016). Erişim tarihi: 20 Mart 2016, http://www.unicef.org/turkey/pc/_cp36.html.

UNICEF (2016). Çocuklar için birleşin. Erişim tarihi: 22 Mart 2016, http://www.unicef.org/turkey/dn_2006/cp43html.

UNICEF, (2012). Türkiye'de çocuk ve genç nüfusun durumunun analizi. Erişim Tarihi 30 Nisan 2016 http://abdigm.meb.gov.tr/projeler/ois/egitim/033.pdf.

Wang, X., Zhou, L. ve Shang, X. (2015). Child poverty in rural China: multi dimensional perspective. *Asian Social Work And Policy Review, 9(2015)*, 109–124.

Wei, Q. W., Zhank, J. X., Scherpbier, R. W., Zhao, C. C., Luo, S. S., Wang, X. L. ve Guo, S. F. (2015). High prevelance of developmental delay among children under three years of ages in poverty-stricken areas of China. *The Royal Society for Public Health, 129*, 1610–1617.

Weinger, S. (1998). Poor children know their place perceptions of poverty class and public messages. *Journal of Sociology and Social Welfare. 15(2)*, 100–118.

Yazıcı, Ö. (2012). Korunmaya muhtaç çocuklar ve çocuk evleri. *Mustafa Kemal Üniversitesi Sosyal Bilimler Enstitüsü Dergisi, 9(18)*, 499–525.

Yazıcıoğlu, Y. ve Erdoğan, S. (2004). *SPSS Uygulamalı Bilimsel Araştırma Yöntemleri*. Detay Yayıncılık: Ankara.

Yıldırım, A. ve Şimşek, H. (2005). *Sosyal bilimlerde nitel araştırma yöntemleri*. Seçkin Yayınevi: Ankara.

Yusufoğlu, Ö. Ş. ve Kızmaz, Z. (2015). Parçalanmış ailelerde yoksulluk ve sosyal dışlanma: Elazığ örneği, *Social Science, 11 (1)*, 27–40.

Zuckerman, B. S. ve Sandel, M. (2013). Bölüm 100: Yoksulluk, evsizlik ve sosyal düzensizlik. M. Yurdakök (Çeviri Editörü), *Rudolph pediatri* (ss. 370–372). Ankara: Güneş Tıp Kitabevleri.

Appendix

Appendix 1. Questionnaire on Mapping the Child Poverty in Mamak

Hello,

This questionnaire has been prepared under the Project *"Mapping of Mamak District Child Poverty"* and is being implemented with the support of the Ankara Development Agency. With the information obtained under the Project, the child poverty situation in the region will try to be described. The prevention of child poverty in the Mamak district will be determined by what can be done. The questionnaire will be completed in consultation with parents that have children. The information obtained under this study will be used only within the scope of the study and personal information obtained from this study will not be shared with others. Your answers to the questions are important for research. Thank you for supporting us in the research.

With Our Respect
Project Team

I. PART: GENERAL INFORMATION

Respondent: Mother ( )   Father ( )

1. How old are you?
1.) 15–25   2.) 26–36   3.) 37–47   4.) 48–58   5.) 59 and older

2. How old is your spouse?
1.) 15–25   2.) 26–36   3.) 37–47   4.) 48–58   5.) 59 and older

3. What is your educational status?
1.) illiterate   2.) literate   3.) primary education   4.) left high school
5.) high school   6.) associate degree   7.) graduated from a university

4. What is your spouse's educational status?
1.) illiterate   2.) literate   3.) primary education   4.) left high school
5.) high school   6.) associate degree   7.) graduated from a university

5. What is your marital status?
1.) married ( ) civil marriage ( ) unofficial wedding   **How many times did you
get married?.........**   2.) divorced (go to 7th question)   3.) widow (go to
7th question)   4.) Other.........

6. How long have you been married?
1.) 1–5   2.) 6–10   3.) 11–15   4.) 16–20   5.) 21 and older

7. How old were you when you married? (after answering go to
    16th question)
1.) 13–17   2.) 18–22   3.) 23–27   4.) 28–32   5.) 33 and older

8. Why did you leave your spouse?
1.) financial problems
2.) unemployment
3.) violence
4.) bad habits
5.) relationship with someone else
6.) Others..

9. Do you receive alimony from your old partner?
1.) Yes   2.) No (go to 12th question)

10. How much do you receive in alimony?
1.) 0–200 TL   2.) 201–400 TL   3.) 401–600 TL   4.) 601 TL and above

11. How long did you stay married?
1.) 1–5   2.) 6–10   3.) 11–15   4.) 16–20   5.) 21 and above

12. Do you receive the orphan's pension?
1.) Yes   2.) No (go to 14th question)

13. How much do you receive from the orphan's pension? (after answering go to 16th question)
1.) 0–200 TL   2.) 201–400 TL   3.) 401–600 TL   4.) 601 TL and above

14. Do you receive the widow's pension?
1.) Yes   2.) No (go to 16th question)

15. How much do you receive widow's pension?
1.) 0–200 TL   2.) 201–400 TL   3.) 401–600 TL   4.) 601 TL and above

16. Where were you born? City: ....
1.) City   2.) Provincial   3.) Village

17. Did you come to where you live due to migration?
1.) Yes   2.) No (go to 21st question)

18. Where did you immigrate from?
1.) Village   2.) Provincial   3.) City   4.) Abroad

19. When did you immigrate?
1.) 0–2 years   2.) 3–5 years   3.) 6–11 years   4.) 12–20 years   5.) 21 and above

20. Why did you immigrate?
1.) Job Opportunities   2.) Children's Education   3.) Marriage   4.) Health Problems
5.) Security   6.) Others..............

21. How many years have you been living in Ankara?
1.) 0–2 years   2.) 3–5 years   3.) 6–11 years   4.) 12–20 years   5.) 21 and above

22. Do you have debts or hire purchases?
1.) Yes [Any legal action was made? Y/N]   2.) No (go to 25th question)

23. How much debt do you have?
1.) 0–500 TL   2.) 501–1500 TL   3.) 1501–3000 TL   4.) 3001–5000 TL
5.) 5001 TL and above

24. To whom do you owe?
1.) Person   2.) Tradesman   3.) Houseowner   4.) Shop   5.) Bank
6.) Invoice   7.) Others..............

25. What is your health insurance?
1.) I don't have any.   2.) Social Insurance Institution   3.) Individual Payment
4.) Retired   5.) Public Health Insurance

26. Do you have a job?
1.) Yes   2.) Retired (go to 28th question)   3.) No (go to 33rd question)

27. What is your job?
1.) Construction Worker   2.) Pitchman   3.) Industrial Worker   4.) Farmer
5.) Tradesman   6.) Driver   7.) Casual Laborer   8.) Handiwork
9.) Childcare   10.) Others............

28. Does your spouse work? (you can encode the above options 27th question)
1.) Yes.....................................   2.) No

29. What is your monthly income?
....

30. Is there any other employee in the family except you and your spouse?
1.) Yes   Specify................   2.) No

31. Where do you first spend the money you earn? (After this question, go to 37th question)
1.) To kitchen costs   2.) To heating   3.) To debt   4.) To children's education
5.) Others.........

32. How long have you been unemployed?
1.) 0–6 months   2.) 7 months–1 year   3.) 1–2 years   4.) 2–3 years
4.) 3 years and above

33. How do you earn your living when you are unemployed?
1.) Family Help   2.) Neighbors Help   3.) Municipality   4.) Foundation
5.) Welfare   6.) Others..........

34. Do you want to work in a job with a regular income?
1.) Yes   2.) No (go to 37th question)

35. Why do you want to work in a job with regular income? (After answering the question, go to 37th question)
1.) To buy what I want   2.) To support my spouse   3.) To get the needs of my children   4.) To pay debts   5.) Others..........

36. Why do you not want to work?
1.) My spouse does not allow   2.) Due to health problems   3.) No one will look after my children   4.) I can not find work   5.) Old age
6.) others..................................

37. Has your spouse ever been unemployed?
1.) yes   2.) No (go to 40th question)   3.) did not work yet

38. How do you make your living, when your spouse is unemployed?
1.) family help   2.) neighbors help   3.) municipality   4.) foundation
5.) welfare   6.) others..

39. What is the average monthly income of the family?
....

40. Is there anyone with health problems in your home?
1.) Yes   2.) No

41. Is there any one treated with continuous medication because of disease?
1.) Yes (Go to the next question)   2.) No (go to the 43rd question)

42. Is medications covered by the state?
1.) yes   2.) no

43. Does your family have people with disabilities?
1.) Yes   2.) No (g oto 46th Question)

44. Do you receive support from the state for people with disabilities in your family?
1.) Yes ( ) 2022 ( ) home care costs   2.) No

45. What is the amount you receive in monthly support for people with disabilities?
1.) 0–200   2.) 201–400   3.) 401–600   4.) 601–800   5.) 801 and above

46. Do you receive medical assistance?
1.) Yes (go to the 48th question)   2.) No

47. Why don't you receive medical assistance?
1.) we don't have health insurance   2.) we don't have time   3.) our financial
opportunities aren't enough   4.) The health clinic is far away   5.) drugs are
expensive   6.) Others...................

48. Did you feel excessively unhappy and depressed last week? How many days?
1.) 0   2.) 1–2   3.) 3–4   4.) 5–7

49. Last year, did you feel yourself extremely sad or depressed or did you lose interest in the things which were you interested in or that you like?.....
1.) Yes   2.) No

50. Did you feel extreme depression or sadness in your life in the last two years?

1.) Yes   2.) No

51. Which of the following types of aid did you benefit from?

1.) shelter   2.) food   3.) clothing   4.) education   5.) health
6.) disability assistance   7.) none of them   8.) others....................

52. Where do you do your shopping for the kitchen?

1.) bazaar   2.) markets   3.) peddler   4.) greengrocer   5.) grocer
6.) others

53. Where do you do your shopping for clothing?

1.) store   2.) bazaar   3.) peddler   4.) 2nd hand   5.) family/neighbor
6.) aid

54. How often do you eat meat products?

1.) almost every day   2.) several times a week   3.) once a week   4.) once
a month   5.) a few times a year 6.) any time

55. How often do you eat dairy products?

1.) Almost every day   2.) Several times a week   3.) Once a week
4.) Once a month   5.) Never

56. How often do you eat vegetables?

1.) Almost every day   2.) Several times a week   3.) Once a week
4.) Once a month 5.) Never

57. How often do you eat fruit?

1.) Almost every day   2.) Several times a week   3.) Once a week
4.) Once a month   5.) Several times a year   6.) Never

II. QUESTIONS ABOUT THE HOUSE

1. What kind of house do you live in?
1.) slum   2.) detached house   3.) apartment   4.) others....................

2. Who owns the house in which you live?
1.) Rent
2.) My own (go to the 4ᵗʰ question)
3.) My family (go to the 4ᵗʰ question)
4.) My spouse's family (go to the 4ᵗʰ question)
5.) A helpful person (go to the 4ᵗʰ question)
6.) Others......................

3. How much rent do you pay monthly?
1.) 0–200 TL   2.) 201–400 TL   3.) 401–600 TL   4.) 601–800 TL
5.) 801 TL and above

4. How many rooms are there in your home (including hall)?
1.) One   2.) Two   3.) Three   4.) Four   5.) Five and Above

5. What is the internal structure of your home? (you can select more than one)
1.) separate kitchen   2.) not separate kitchen   3.) separate bathroom
4.) bathroom and toilet together   5.) toilet inside   6.) toilet outside

6. Which of the following electronic items are available in your house?

	Have	Have Not
1.) refrigerator	( )	( )
2.) television	( )	( )
3.) washing machine	( )	( )
4.) computer	( )	( )
5.) iron	( )	( )
6.) telephone	( )	( )
7.) oven	( )	( )
8.) dishwasher	( )	( )
9.) vacuum cleaner	( )	( )
10.) combi-boiler	( )	( )
11.) mobile phone (How many.....)	( )	( )
12.) tablet computer (How many.....)	( )	( )

7. Do you have any relatives living with you except your spouse and kids?
1.) Yes   2.) No (Go to 9th question)

8. Who lives with you?
1.) my mother and father   2.) my spouse's father and mother   3.) sister or brother   4.) my spouse's sister and brother   5.) aunts   6.) uncles
7.) grandmother/grandfather   8.) Others.................................

9. How many people live in the household?
....

10. How do you provide for your heating needs?
1.) natural gas   2.) electricity   3.) wood   4.) Coal   5.) Other

11. What do you use for warming?
1.) Stove   2.) central heating   3.) combi boiler   4.) Others.....................

12. How do you supply your need for drinking water?
1.) tap water at home   2.) out of home tap water   3.) fountain outside
4.) box   5.) other

13. How do you cook your meal?
1.) bottled gas   2.) natural gas   3.) electricity   4.) wood   5.) coal
6.) Others..............

14. What are your complaints about your home? (you can select more than one)
1.) Inadequate number of rooms   2.) Cold   3.) Damp   4.) The lack of toiletries or bathroom   5.) Security issue   6.) Insect / mouse   7.) Little enlightenment   8.) Others................

15. How many times have you changed homes in the last two years?
....

16. Do you leave your children under the age of 12 alone at home without an adult?
1.) Yes   2.) No

CHAPTER III. INTERVIEW FOR CHILDREN

1. How many children do you have?
1.) One   2.) Two   3.) Three   4.) Four   5.) Five and above

2. What's your children's gender? How old are your children? What is your child learning situation?

	Gender	Age	Date of birth	Learning situation
1. Child				
2. Child				
3. Child				
4. Child				
5. Child				
6. Child				
7. Child				
8. Child				
9. Child				

3. Do your children have health insurance?
1.) Yes   2.) No (go to the 5th question)

4. What is your children's health insurance?
1.) Social Insurance Institution   2.) Bağkur   3.) Pension Fund   4.) Green Card

5. Did you have a child who died after being born?
1.) Yes   2.) No

6. How many times have you or your spouse undergone health checks during pregnancy?
1.) once a month   2.) 3–6 times   3.) 1–2 times   4.) never

7. How many times did your last child have a checkup when she or he was in infancy (0–12 months)?
1.) once a month   2.) once in 2–3 months   3.) once in 4–8 months
4.) once a year   5.) never

8. Did you get your children's vaccines regularly?
1.) Yes   2.) No

9. Do you take your children to a health center when she or he have a health problem?
1.) Yes   2.) No

10. Do your children have an important disease?
1.) Yes (What?.....................................)   2.) No

11. Do your children have a health problem which is untreated?
1.) Yes (What.....................................)   2.) No

12. Do your children have a health problem related with not enough nutrition?
1.) Yes (What.....................................)   2.) No

13. Do you have a disabled child? If you have, how many?
1.) Yes (species barrier: ....) - (How many.........................)
2.) No

14. How many meals do your children eat?
1.) Three   2.) Two   3.) One   4.) Others.................

15. Did your children start elementary school on time?
1.) Yes   2.) No (How many........)

16. Did your children get a pre-school education?
1.) Yes   2.) No (How many children didn't get? .....) (go to 18th question)

17. How many years did your children get pre-school education?
1.) 0–1 year   2.) 2–3 years   3.) 4 years and above

18. Do you have any children who did not attend a school although she or he is of compulsory school age?
1.) Yes (How many.....)   2.) No (go to 23rd question)

19. How many children do you have who can not attend primary school? (Please indicate the number of children).....................................

20. How many children do you have who can not attend secondary school? (Please indicate the number of children).....................................

21. How many children do you have who can not attend high school? (Please indicate the number of children).....................................

22. What are the reasons that your children can not go to school?
1.) Financial difficulties   2.) He/she does not want to go to school   3.) He/she has to work   4.) Others.................

23. Does your child continue regular training? If the answer is no, why?
1.) Yes   2.) No (Why...)

24. Are you able to supply the training needs of your children like tools, school uniform, travel costs, etc.
1.) Yes   2.) No

25. How much money do you spend per month for your children's education?
.... TL

26. What do you spend your money mostly on when it comes to the education of your children?
1.) school allowance   2.) stationery (like boks)   3.) school bus fee
4.) school fees   5.) clothing, etc.   6.) Others.............................

27. Do you receive support to supply the educational needs of your children?
1.) Yes   2.) No (go to 29. question)

28. Where do you get support to meet the educational needs of your children?
1.) Family/ relatives   2.) School   3.) Social assistance and solidarity foundation
4.) Municipality   5.) Other foundations / associations

29. Do you prefer your children to work or to read?
1.) to read (go to 31st question)   2.) to work

30. Why do you prefer your children to work?
1.) Because we need money   2.) To learn and have a job   3.) Others.........

31. Do you think it will be a benefit to your family in the future to have your child receive a good education?
1.) Yes   2.) No

32. What kind of benefit will you have when your children get an education?
1.) Get a job easy   2.) They look after us when we get old   3.) Become a knowledgeable people

33. What can you not buy which your children need?
1.) Compute   2.) Toys   3.) Clothes   4.) Foods   5.) Telephone
6.) Nothing   7.) Medicine   8.) Others......

34. Do you give pocket money to your children?
1.) Yes   2.) No (go to 36th question)

35. How much money do you give each child per day?
1.) 0–1 TL   2.) 2–3 TL   3.) 4–5 TL   4.) 6–7 TL   5.) 8 TL and above

36. Do you have a child who is working?
1.) Yes   2.) No (go to 45th question)

37. What is his/her job?

1.) Working as mechanic   2.) Working in cafe/restaurant   3.) Working in barbershop/hairdresser   4.) Working in the market/bazaar   5.) Casual works   6.) Shoe shiners   7.) Sells wipes/pastry   8.) Collecting paper waste   9.) Others......................

38. How long has he/she been working? You can select more than one. Please indicate the number of children.

1.) 4–7   2.) 8–11   3.) 12–15   4.) 16–19   5.) 20 and above

39. How many hours does she/he work a day? You can select more than one. Please indicate the number of children

1.) 0–3   2.) 4–7   3.) 8–11   4.) 12 and above

40. How many hours does she/he work a week? You can select more than one. Please indicate the number of children

1.) 0–5   2.) 6–15   3.) 16–25   4.) 26–35   5.) 36 and above

41. When does she/he work? You can select more than one. Please indicate the number of children

1.) After school   2.) On weekends   3.) Summer holiday   4.) Everyday because she/he does not go to school

42. What does he/she do with the money he/she earns? You can select more than one. Please indicate the number of children

1.) Support the household needs   2.) Earn a school allowance   3.) Others......................

43. Does he/she like his job? Please indicate for each child

1.) Yes   2.) No

44. Were there anything upsetting or scary to him / her at work? Please indicate for each child

1.) Yes (What................................)   2.) No

45. How do his/her school friends behave towards her/him? Please indicate for each child.

1.) Good   2.) Bad

46. Is your child able to find the time to play or spend time with his/her friends? Please indicate for each child.

1.) Yes   2.) No

47. Are there any moments when your children does not come home or spend the night on the street? Please indicate for each child.
1.) Yes   2.) No (go to 49th question)

48. How long does your child not come home without notice? Please indicate for each child.
1.) One day   2.) A few days   3.) One to two weeks   4.) One to two months

49. Do your children have friends living/working on the streets? Please indicate for each child.
1.) Yes   2.) No

50. Does your child have bad habits? Please indicate for each child.
1.) Yes   2.) No (go to 52nd question)

51. What kind of bad habits does she/he has? Please indicate for each child.
1.) Lie   2.) Theft   3.) Use of the volatiles   4.) Cigarette
5.) Using alcohol   6.) Running away from home   7.) Others.......................

52. Have your children been involved in a crime before? Please indicate for each child.
1.) Yes   2.) No (Go to 54th question)

53. Was she/he punished from this crime? Please indicate for each child.
1.) Yes   2.) No

54. How do you treat your children when he/she does something wrong?
1.) We beat   2.) We get angry and yell   3.) We ignore   4.) We talking about the wrong   5.) Others.........................

55. Do you have a child adopted or taken under protection of state?
1.) Yes (Gender and age)................................   2.) No

56. Do your children have a room of their own?
1.) Yes   2.) No

57. Do your children have toys of their own?
1.) Yes   2.) No

58. How many hours do your children watch TV a day?
....

59. Do you think that your children are eating healthy?
1.) Yes   2.) No

60. Does your child want things that are hard to supply for them?
1.) Yes   2.) No (go to 64th question)

61. What does your child want that are hard for you to supply?
1.) Food   2.) Needs related to education   3.) Computer / mobile phone
4.) Clothes   5.) Travel/go on a holiday   6.) Others...............................

62. How do your children react when you can not supply their demands?
1.) Cry / get upset   2.) Make comparisons   3.) Vomit   4.) Blame us
5.) Behaving reasonably   6.) Others....................

63. Do you have any concerns about the future of your children?
1.) Yes   2.) No (Go to 65th question)

64. What kind of concerns do you have about the future of your children?
....

65. What do you think about poverty?...

SURVEY OVER, THANK YOU!

CONTROL LIST

PRE- POLL			
Will Be Held	*Yes*	*No*	*Explanation*
Have you received an appointment to the survey?			
Have you confirmed the appointment a day before going to the polls?			
Did you give any information about the content and process of the survey?			
Did you get familiar with the questionnaire?			
Did you think on the examples to make questions' meanings stronger?			
Did you prepare a notebook to record different situations?			
Did you review your note-taking method?			
Have you been to where the survey will be made at least half an hour ago?			

During Survey Application			
Will be performed	*Yes*	*No*	*Explanation*
Did you turn down the volume on your phone?			
Did you introduce yourself?			
Did you reserve enough time to meet?			
Did you explain the purpose and scope of the survey?			
Did you select the questions to ask?			
Have you checked all the questions that you ask?			
Did you answer the questions of the people interviewed?			
Did you do everything to remain focused on the study?			
Did you ask whether there is another question before the end of the interview?			
Did you get the necessary additional documents before the end of the survey?			

After Survey			
Will be performed	*Yes*	*No*	*Explanation*
Have you checked the documents you need to take?			
Did you order all of the files in the survey?			
Did you check whether any unwanted questions in the survey?			

Appendix 2. Mamak District Child Poverty Mapping – Interview Guide

VOLUNTARY INFORMED CONSENT

Dear Participant,

The study on the Mamak Town Child Poverty Mapping Survey which is conducted by the Ankara University and supported by the Ankara Development Agency, it aim is to describe the depth of child poverty, reasons for child poverty, and provide a submission of solutions. Fort he scope of the research, you are required to allocate approximately 30 minutes. During the interview, audio recording will be performed. Participation in this study is completely voluntary. Answering the questions in full, without influence from others, is the most convenient way for you to achieve the goals of the study. Reading and approving this form will mean that you agree to participate in this research. The information obtained under this study will be used only within the study and your personal information will be kept confidential. If you need more information beyond this information given about the purpose of the research, you can ask your questions at the end of interview or now to the researcher.

I read the above information and the information must be given to participants before the study and I understand the scope and purpose of the intended study and the responsibilities incumbent on us as a volunteer. Written and verbal explanation was made about the study by the researcher whose name is written below. The potential risks of the study were spoken to me and it was announced there will not be loss of meaning or no contributions because of empty questions. Enough confidence was given to me that my personal information would be protected.

In these conditions I agree to voluntarily participate in the study mentioned without pressure and indoctrination and I agree to my voice being recorded.

The participants'
Name:
Surname:...
Signature:

Communication information:

E-mail: Telephone:

152

INTERVIEW GUIDE ABOUT MAMAK DISTRICT MAPPING OF CHILD POVERTY

This guide is intended under the Project of Mamak District Mapping of Child Poverty which is carried out with the support of the Ankara Development Agency and its purposes are about child poverty status at Mamak district and the prevention of child poverty, to clarify the boundaries of individual interviews with children and parents and it is intended in a healthy way to ensure the collection of data through standard forms.

Located Forms In The guide
☐ Family Individual Interview Form
☐ Children Individual Interview Form
☐ Checklists

Family Individual Interview Form

1- General Information About Interview
a- Information about the Family

Mother / Father's Name and Last Name	
Age	
Educational Status	
His/Her job	
Job Year	
Telephone (job/ cell)	
E-mail:	

b- Information about Interview Performer Expert

Name- Surname	
Telephone:	
E-Mail:	

c- Information about Interview

Interview Date	
Interview Place	
Interview Start - Finish Time	
Interview Duration	

d- Information about the Interview Record
- ☐ allowed to voice record
- ☐ not allowed to voice record

2- Interview Questions

1. Do you have any poor people around you? Could you define poverty for me?
2. How does your daily life go? Can you tell me your 'one day'?
3. Do you get help from anywhere to meet your needs except social assistance and the solidarity foundation? If you get help, where do you get help? Is this assistance sufficient for you?
4. They come to examine your house from the foundation. Are you satisfied with the attitude and behavior of people who come from the foundation? Do they treat you well?
5. What type of needs can you not meet that your children have?
6. What do you do to meet them?
7. What can you not buy for your children even though your children want it?
8. How do you feel when you can not buy your children's wants?
9. Are there any disruption in your child's education because of poverty?
10. How does your child react when you can not meet their desires from school?
11. Are there any disruption in your child's health because of poverty?
12. Are there any times you can not buy medicine when your child is sick?
13. Is your child being fed enough? Does your child eat meat, milk, eggs?
14. Where do you do your food shopping? Do you collect food waste from the bazaar or markets?
15. If you have enough income, what environment would you like to live in?
16. What are your expectations about the future of your family? Do you ever feel unsafe for the future? If you feel unsafe, what issues do you feel unsafe about?
17. What would you do if you had a magic wand in your hand?
18. What is your opinion about to stop poverty in a society?
19. If you have a chance to born again, what do you want to change about yourself?

20. If you have a chance to born again, what do you want to change about society?

* Suggested ways to eliminating risks

If the purpose of the research and borders are specified clearly at the beginning of the interview, the risk of detection can be controlled about the interview's audit process

Children Individual Interview Form

1- General Information About Interview

a- Information about the child

Name-Surname	
Gender	
Age	
Class	

b- Information about Interview Performer Expert

Name-Surname	
Telephone	
E-Mail	

c- Information about interview

Interview Date	
Interview Place	
Interview Start - Finish Time	
Interview Duration	

d- Information about the Interview Record

☐ allowed to voice record

☐ not allowed to voice record

2- Interview Questions

1. Do you have any poor people around you? Could you define poverty to me?
2. How does your an average day? When you get up in the morning, what do you do during the day, when you sleep at night?
3. What can you not get even though you want it?
4. How do you feel when you can not get what you want?
5. Do you argue with your family about money?

6. Can your parents give you a regular allowance? Is this enough money for you?
7. How do you spend the money given by your family?
8. Are there any poor children among your friends? Do you share your allowance with your friends when you get it?
9. Do you share your food with your friends?
10. How do you feel when you see your wants in your friends?
11. Can you meet your school needs? How do you feel when you can not meet your school needs?
12. Does the director or teacher get angry at you when you can not meet your school needs? How do they behave?
13. Do you go to the doctor when you are sick? Can you buy and take the medicine when the doctor suggests medication?
14. Which job do you want to perform in the future?
15. What would you do if you had a magic wand in your hand?
16. If you have a chance to born again, what do you want to change about yourself and your family?
17. If you have a chance to born again, what do you want to change about the society?

* Risks that might prevent the negotiations to achieve the desired goal:
  – *Risk of not understandable questions*
  – *Risk of some concepts being unknown*
* Suggested ways to eliminating risks
  – *According to the differences in cognitive maturity, to control the risk of not understandable questions, some examples (quality will not result in manipulation) prepared before giving to children, may lead them to think the desirable possible answer to the question*

Pre-Interview Individual interviews			
Will be performed	Yes	No	Explanation
Did you get an appointment for an interview?			
Have you confirmed the appointment a day before going to the polls?			
Did you give information about content and process?			
Did you give information to the director about features of meeting room?			
Have you previously provided contact information for the teaching staff?			

Did you find out the exact address of the institution and transportation alternatives?			
Did you become familiar with the interview questions?			
Did you think about examples to promote understanding of interview questions?			
Have you prepared the interview audio recording confirmation form?			
Is your voice recorder ready?			
Have you checked the battery of the audio recording device?			
Did you supply a backup battery for your audio recording device?			
Have you tested the recording performance of the audio recording device?			
Have you checked if there is enough space in the memory of the audio recording device?			
Have you prepared the notebook?			
Did you review your own note keeping ways?			
Have you been to institution at least half an hour ago?			

During the interview individual interviews			
Will be performed	Yes	No	Explanation
Did you turn down the volume on your phone?			
Have you received approval for voice recording?			
Did you introduce yourself?			
Did you reserve enough time to meet?			
Did you explain the purpose and scope of the survey?			
Did you select the questions you ask?			
Have you checked all the questions that you ask?			
Did you answer the questions of the people interviewed?			
Did you do everything to remain focused on the study?			
Did you check that the recording of the voice recorder during the interview?			
Did you ask whether there is another question before the end of the interview			
Did you get the necessary additional documents before the end of the survey?			

Post-Interview Individual interviews / focus group interviews			
Will be performed	Yes	No	Explanation
Have you checked that audio record worked?			
Have you checked the documents you need to take?			
Did you transfare the voice recording to your computer?			

Appendix 3. Asked Questions Scope Workshop

- What is Child Poverty?
- What are the studies related to Child Poverty in Turkey?
- What are the facts of problems related to Child Poverty?
- What are the solution proposals about Child Povery?
- Which of the solution proposals can be performed in the short term and which of the solution proposals can be performed in the long term and which organizations can perform them?

Appendix 4. Swot Analysis

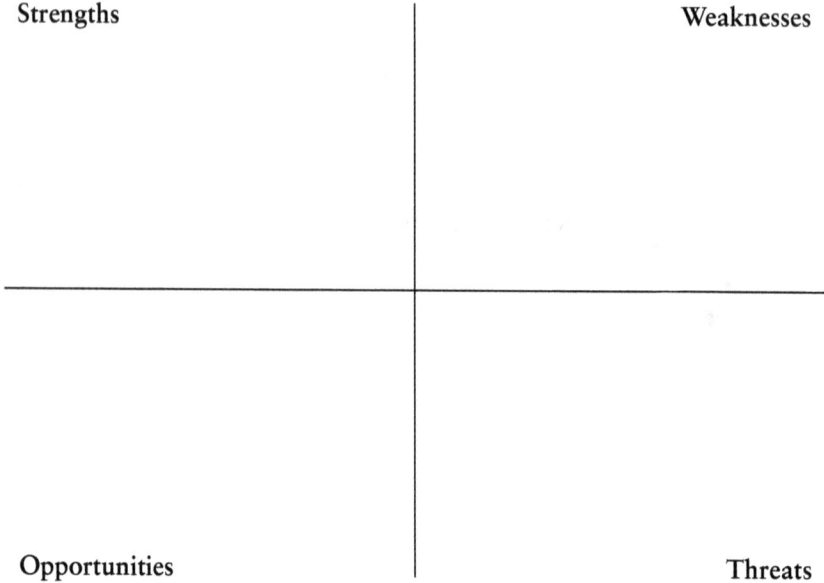

Strengths   Weaknesses

Opportunities   Threats

Appendix 5. Workshop Report

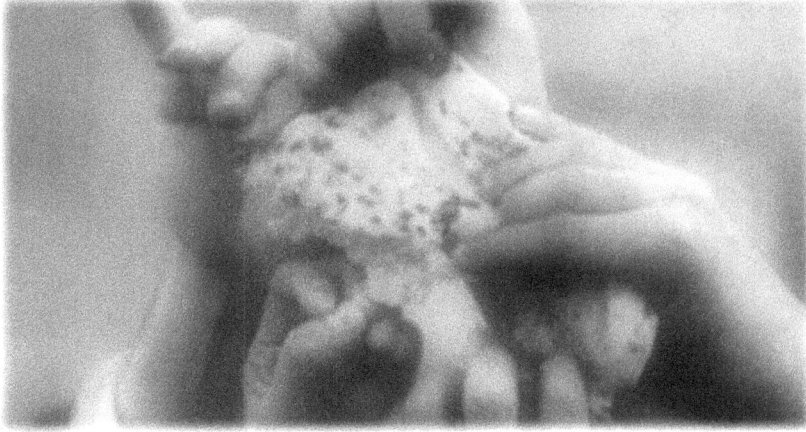

Kaynak: http://www.haber5.com/guncel/yoksul-cocugun-ailesine-denetim

Ankara/2016

After the the completion of the data collection and analysis processes about the Mamak Child Poverty Mapping Project which is supported by the Ankara Development Agencies and executed by Coordinator of Child Science Centre Prof. Dr. Neriman Aral the project workshop was held with the following program on 15.04.2016, in Büyük Sürmeli Otel.

09:00–09:30: Registration

Welcome and registration was made for the workshop at 09.00–09.30. Teachers, doctor, village headmen, child development experts, social workers, academics, provincial migration expert, and municipal officials participated in the workshop who are working with children in the Mamak region. In total 51 participants attended the workshop.

09:30–09:45: OPENING

After completion of the registration process, the opening was performed with a moment of silence and the National Anthem, and then information was given about studies to be carried during the day.

**09:45–10:15 CHILDREN'S UNIVERSITY AND PROJECT IDENTIFI-
CATION**

Exp. Ece ÖZDOĞAN ÖZBAL from Children's University, has announced
the launch of the center accompanied by a video about the Children's University

After the presentation of Coordination Of Child Science Centre, Coordinator Prof. Dr. Neriman ARAL gave information about the output of
the project objectives, targets, sustainability, studies so far, studies to be
carried out after and introducing the project team she explained the work
to be done under the project.

10:15–10:40: PRESENTATION OF PROJECT RESULTS
Exp. Sebahat AYDOS gave information about the results of the work carried out under the Project.

Some of the striking results which are achieved by analyzing the data obtained through interviews with the participants face to face by going to 408 households under the project was shared with the workshop participants. The results of in-depth interviews with mothers and children was shared too. A break was provided in the direction of the program and then the group working started.

11.00–12.30: GROUP WORKING
Participants were divided into three groups according to predetermined criteria. Each group located different professions elements. Groups worked at the table prepared for them and established a leader and reporter. In the morning session, the participants sought answers to the following questions

- What is Child Poverty?
- What are the studies related to Child Poverty in Turkey?
- What are the facts of problems related to Child Poverty?
- What are the solution proposals about Child Poverty?

- Which of the solution proposals should be performed in the short term and which of the solution proposals should be performed in the long term and which organizations can perform them?

Each participant in the groups discussed these questions regarding their working conditions, and the functions of their departments and agencies. Each participating institution had the opportunity to learn about the other institutions. The participants continued their group work after lunch.

13:30–15:00: GROUP WORKING 2

In the afternoon session a SWOT Analysis was conducted regarding Child Poverty.

Participants in the group discussed the strengths and weaknesses of Child Poverty. They discussed what can be strengths, who can be affected positively from these strengths, what is the weak side and for whom it formed the weak side. Threat of Child Poverty were discussed in socially and individually dimensions and then the session was completed.

15:30–16:30: PRESENTATIONS OF THE GROUP

After completion of group work, groups shared the reports they generated as a result of discussions in the morning session and the afternoon session with the participants. Presented by each group are the adopted reports written below.

1ˢᵗ GROUP 1ˢᵗ SESSION

What Is Child Poverty?

- The situation is unable to have, unable to reach, or an inability to fully benefit from the most basic rights of children.
- The situation is not benefiting enough from the children's rights like health, nutrition, shelter, safety, education and development.
- Children are exposed to a situation arising from family. Children can not choose poverty. They only assumes the poverty of their family.

If children feel poor, especially social exclusion can be observed. These influences are much more experienced in the school environment at times like feeding time. If children's families are poor, children's work possibilities increase at a very early age. These children may be unable to continue school. Child Poverty is not experienced only in the material sense, because children have not only material needs. As well as financial difficulties, Child Poverty is experienced socially, culturally, and through emotional deprivation. Although some children don't have financial problems, they can live in poverty. Poverty of the family can also affect the quality of communication between family and child.

As a different perspective, children living in poverty have difficulty understanding the difference between good touch and bad touch. They can not have a sense of the difference between malicious push and cuddling for good. A greater likelihood of violence is thought to exist for those living with Child Poverty. Child Poverty is growing like a snowball and affects so many people.

It is observed that children living with poverty want very little for themselves. This can be interpreted as learned helplessness.

• *What are the studies related to Child Poverty in Turkey?*
By the Ministry of Family and Social Policy, social and economic support is given to the families which have children in need of protection. Also within the ministry they have social support programs provided by professional staff that are available in the ministry. A package of programs for families

are also available. Also if parents have the child in need of protection, ministry gives free pre-school education opportunities to the children.

Within the Mamak Municipality, there is active work for children to be directed to sports. At the same time expenditure items are available to meet the children's education and general requirements. Food assistance is made occasionally. Assistances are made for such items as stationery and clothes for school too.

Kızılay's psychosocial support activities are in the foreground. Especially in disaster situations, psychosocial support and therapy work can be done by social workers and psychologists in troubled places. In partnership with the Ministry of Justice, it is being studied the victims of crime and children driven to crime. Training homes are established for children in prison and the needs of these homes are covered by Kızılay. Children in prison are provided to continue their normal schooling. Financial support is provided to families who have a child in prison and that can not go to visit their children because of financial impossibilities. Financial support is provided to children who were released and can not return their homes because of lack of money. Special education classes are set up in schools that are connected to the Ministry of National Education and the needs of this class are covered by Kızılay. With the Love Bundle Project which has been carried out since 2010, children born in families with needs and their mothers needs are met, and then psycho-social support is given to the family afterwards by professional staff. "Love Bazaars" are established in various places. Children can get stuff according to their needs and size from Love Bazaars without paying any money. Red Crescent has owned community centers. Social supports are given for children and their parents after the disaster both nationally and internationally. Mobile child -friendly spaces are created on demand. This system is for Syrian children currently. It is a method used for children who are exposed to hazards in the event of a disaster.

In addition to the institutions help is done to prevent Child Poverty by small groups in society. Companies and brands also help like like institutions.

What are the facts of problems related to Child Poverty?

- The presence of duplicate aid throughout the country, hinders giving aid to a person who has a need, as needed.
- There is a lack of coordination in institutions and between institutions.

- Thanks to media especially in childrens' values' and the way of perceive of themselves are degenerating.
- The problem is stated as the problem of the overall system, when only a single field evaluation like education or health, false conclusions can be reached.
- It does not give the correct results because of assessments and criteria are made with numbers.

What are the solution proposals about child povery?
Proposals To Be Made In The Short Term

- The activities for voluntary work should be increased in schools. – **Ministry of National Education**
- Teachers who educate children, should be evaluated that are appropriate for the job. – **Ministry of National Education**
- The existing system should be provided fairly. – **Goverment**
- Resources allocated to those without the need, should be transferred to those in need. – **Goverment**
- Projects for social services in schools should be increased. – **Ministry of Family And Social Policy and Ministry of National Education**
- Community service should be increased. – **Ministry of National Education and Universities**
- Trainings for women's employment and training centers for women's employment will be open. – **Ministry Of Family And Social Policy**

Proposals To Be Made In The Long Term

- Orphanages should be closed and children's homes system should be extended. – **Ministry Of Family And Social Policy**
- Teachers' hardware should be increased, children's education should not only be for the course, children should be ensured in areas like communication drama. – **Ministry of National Education**
- New support policies should be carried out for the elimination of poverty. – **Ministry Of Family And Social Policy and Ministry of National Education**
- All the assistance given by the government and institutions should be collected in one place. – **Ministry Of Family And Social Policy**

- Legislation should be rearranged and secondary vocational schools should to be opened. – **Ministry of National Education**
- Teachers and professional staff who will work with children should be selected by professionals, paid teacher system should be removed. – **Ministry of National Education**
- Community centers should be established for the training of the family. Municipality should give support to these centers with infrastructure and the execution of these institutions must be ensured with staff support of Ministry of Family and Social Policy. – **Municipalities and Ministry Of Family And Social Policy**
- Loans and lending policies should be changed. – **Banking Regulation and Supervision Agency**
- Centers for street children and child - youth centers must be organized and open. These centers in neighborhoods and community centers which are for children who can receive education and which support children's social development should be expanded – **Ministry Of Family And Social Policy**
- Pre-school education should be free especially in socially disadvantaged areas and a system should be established which meet their food needs. Pre-school education should be made compulsory again. Education must be handled in cooperation with the family. – **Ministry of National Education**
- Education is a system starting from the family. Therefore, family education should be done. Family's hardware should be increased and awareness of family should be increased. – **Ministry of National Education and Ministry Of Family And Social Policy**
- Children should be guided o a job, to an art or to a craft based on their abilities. – **Ministry of National Education**
- The education system need to be clarified – **Ministry of National Education**
- Giving financial support to the family should be considered a final solution, solution-oriented work should be increased like increasing employment opportunities. – **Goverment**
- Serious policies should be developed for the training of the family. – **Ministry of National Education and Ministry Of Family And Social Policy**

- New regulations for the status of children in the justice system should be done and special places should be created for them. – **Ministry of Justice**
- Social support systems in the neighborhood should be increased, places that children can get preschool education should be done at courses for mothers. – **Municipalities and Ministry of National Education**
- Helps should be identified for need. – **Ministry Of Family And Social Policy and Prefectures**

1st GROUP 2nd SESSION

Strengths of Child Poverty:

- Children are away from technology addiction.
- Sharing feelings are experienced more intensely on children.
- Prevention of family poverty on children.
- Children can get access easier to the benefits for themselves.
- Children's feelings are fed about being a good parent.
- Children realize the truth about life at an early age.
- Laws and regulations are adequate at the system in order to resolve Child Poverty.
- Children better know the value of the facilities at hand. They can use their creativity actively in impossibilities.

Weaknesses Of Child Poverty:

- Application of existing laws and regulations is not sufficient.
- Family education of the group living with Child Poverty is generally low.
- The social conditions in which children live in is insufficient.
- Difficulties are experienced in providing continual education.
- There is a high propensity for violence within the family.
- There is a matter of increasing social problems.

Opportunities of Child Poverty

- Any opportunities can not be found about Child Poverty.

Threats Relating to Child Poverty

- People with low self-esteem are increased.
- The crime trends / crime rate are increased.

- The situation of learned helplessness is experienced, children are prevented positive behavior observations.
- Negative social environment is increased.
- The corruption of values being experienced.
- It forms the basis of adult poverty.
- Marriage at an early age / secondary marriage is experienced intensely.
- The use of drugs is increasing.
- Child labor is increasing.
- Divorce is increasing.
- Security threat is experienced intensely.
- Participation in criminal organizations is increasing.
- It causes children to be maliciously used (prostitution, organ mafia, etc.).
- It leads to gender discrimination.
- Because of the normalization of the situation created by the media, the view of social problems are increasing.

2ⁿᵈ GROUP 1ˢᵗ SESSION
What is Child Poverty?

- It is a situation of failure to meet the needs, difficulties in access to resources.
- The fact that children are poor is due to the family's poverty.

- Poverty is economic based but in addition to material poverty, Child Poverty can be understood as a lack of love.
- There is also a lack of social and cultural activities, failure to take effective health services.

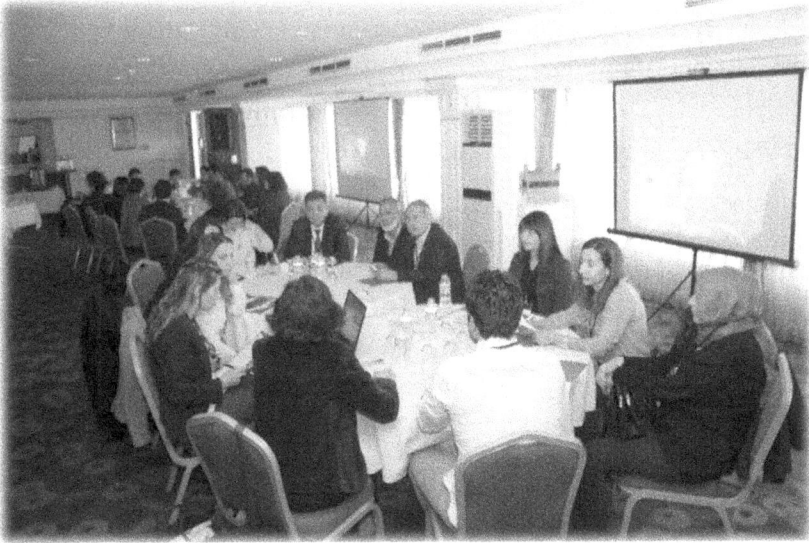

What are the studies related to Child Poverty in Turkey?

Social and economic support is provided by the ministry of family and social policies. This assistance is provided to vulnerable children, to remain in the family and to not go to orphanages. This work is planned to be supported by the Family Support Program (ASDEP). Family counseling services are provided to all families at risk by institution staff. A family meeting is held every three months with social worker. Disabled home care assistance is another type of support.

Conditional Training Assistance is made by the Social Assistance and Solidarity Foundation to children who continue their education, if the child does not attend three and a half days per month, this aid is deducted. Conditional health aid is given to pre-school children. In this health aid, family pay a fee for regular controls every three months. Under the law 2022, families with disabled children receive a salary for three months. It is a paid monthly salary that goes to the soldiers' needy children. Orphans are given a monthly salary.

The aid from Red Crescent, Conditional Training assistance, municipalities, societies, General Directorate of Foundations, and the Ministry of Family and Social Policies are directed to those in need by village headmens.

Ministry of National Education, Stationery support is made by the district national education directorate. Philanthropists can help through the school.

What are the facts about the problems of Child Poverty?

- Domestic violence is observed frequently.
- It is seen that there is involvement in delinquency and crime especially after primary school, children are not punished because of their age and children are released. For this reason, children can develop a sense of motivation and repetition of the same crime is increasing. Counseling Measures decided by the Child Protection Law may be inadequate.
- Early marriage cases are confronted.
- Broken families are increasing.
- Both children and other members of the family have psychological problems.
- There is decrease in children's working habits and willingness to work.
- Drug addiction and drug sales rates are increasing.
- Children are more likely to live on the street.
- There is the possibility of abuse and neglect in every sense.
- Growth retardation has a high incidence.
- Nutrition-related problems can be experienced often.
- Problems relating to the lack of stimulus can be shown.
- Street Work is confronted.
- Children feel negative emotions; such as, feeling worthless, low self esteem.

What are the solution proposals about Child Poverty?
Proposals To Be Made In The Short Term

- Grants must be not only for economic support but also psychological and educational support – **Municipalities, Universities, Ministries**

- Houses of the families should be visited, family education should be increased – **Municipalities, Universities, Ministries, Ministry of District**
- Aid should be distributed according to need. For example, not given sugar to diabetics. – **All organizations that help**
- Two disadvantaged groups can be brought together. For example, a young woman who gets help can clean someone's home who is very old. – **All organizations that help**
- Social Assistance Information System can be use affective by all aid agencies – **All organizations that help**
- Professional people should conduct a detailed examination of the house – **All organizations that help**
- Help should be given to the people who are really in need – **All organizations that help**
- Help criteria should be determined clearly. – **All organizations that help**
- It should be determined that the aid is used for its true aim or not – **All organizations that help**

Proposals To Be Made In The Long Term

- Non-governmental organizations and government agencies do not communicate with each other. therefore it leads to wasted public resources. To prevent this aid should be received from a single source. – **Ministries**
- People don't want to get a job because when they get a job, their help will be cut. These people should be provided with participation in the labor force in their home environment – **Ministries.**
- Without distinction different cultures, income levels and denominations, families should be placed in the way they socialize to provide social learning and model taking learning. – **Municipalities and Ministries.**
- Families from socially disadvantaged environments should not be placed in the same environment groups – **Municipalities and Ministries**
- Education policies should be well identified and children should be raised with work ethics – **Ministries**
- There should be facilitated access to service centers – **Municipalities and Ministries**

2nd GROUP 2nd SESSION

Strengths of Child Poverty:

- There is ease of access to social assistance.
- Helping poor people is at the forefront.
- Gains can be obtained from without having a job.
- Problem-solving skills are higher.
- Coping with stress and confronting challenges capacity is high.
- Government agencies and civil society organizations draw attention to these areas much more.
- It is the focus of interest of the university.
- Problems are not experienced in finding help resources.
- Children under 18 are under guarantee with legislation.
- The children are besides their mother constantly.
- Solidarity and sharing behavior are high.

Weaknesses of the Child Poverty:

- Job satisfaction can not be achieved.
- The rate of turning to crime is high.
- Not contributing to production.
- Lack of confidence is experienced intensely.
- There is no cooperation between aid agencies.
- The data obtained in the field does not comply with the policy.
- There are no dissuasive elements.
- People are accustomed to meeting the needs without having a job.
- Children's education is interrupted.
- Poverty is learned helplessness and the children have adopted it.
- There are no positive role models for children.
- There is no health and education consciousness.
- There is a lack of sanctions.
- Aid does not meet with who has real needs everytime.
- Fieldworkers' opinions and recommendations are not demanded when the national policies are creating.
- Educational support is not given enough to the families.
- Play areas and social activity areas are inadequate.

Opportunities Related to Child Poverty:

- Poverty is used for getting money.
- It is a policy material for election time.
- Problems are detected with studies.
- It constitutes grounds to the creation of new government policies.
- State makes a claim to the problems.
- Increasing the awareness of society.
- Service is taken to the families by experienced professionals.

Threats Relating to Child Poverty:

- Aid increase the likelihood of migration.
- Children are open to abuse and neglect.
- Early age marriage possibility is high.
- There is a possibility of internal and external migration.
- Crime and using drug possibilities are high.
- The possibility of involving children in criminal organizations is increasing.
- Children are available to run on the street.
- Children's growth and development are at risk.
- Children's education is interrupted.
- There is no social consciousness.
- Children in poverty constitutes cheap labor.
- Poverty affects children's friendships.
- Parents are unemployed, families have socio-economic problems, employment opportunities are limited.
- The position of serving staff about wear out.
- There is the possibility of misuse of aid and this situation leads to loss of labor and material loss.
- Parental education is low, and parental skills are weak.
- Some civil society organizations are using poverty for an unethical income.

3ʳᵈ GROUP 1ˢᵗ SESSION

What is Child Poverty?

- Child Poverty is based on the increase of family poverty.
- When one says Child Poverty, non-conscious parents not interested enough with their children comes to mind.
- Fathers remain in the background of their family and does not deal with children. Or due to being unemployed long-term and upset with the amount of aid, fathers can cause violence to their children or spouse.

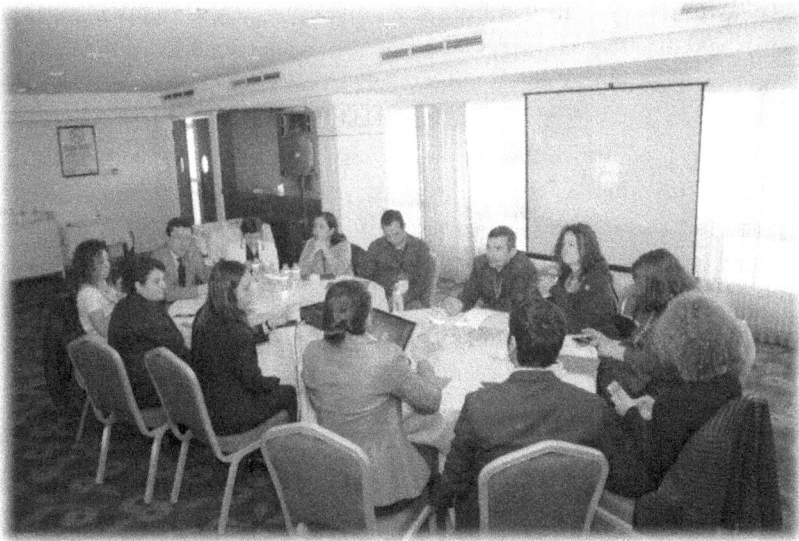

What are the studies related to Child Poverty in Turkey?
Home care services are provided by Family and Social Policy Minister. Long-term socio-economic help is available for one or two years. Mothers were given training and given the opportunity to obtain a job in public and women's centers, which were available within the ministry until 2010. At the same time, at these centers, pre-school education services were given to preschool children, study service was given to the school age children including two groups morning and afternoon, and there was a computer library (these centers were closed in 2010). Preventive protective measures are available in the neighborhood. If necessary, pre-school educational support services are provided by the ministry. As for the families whose children have disabilities, there are temporary "guest care" institutions. Here, families can leave their disabled children for free to the institution where 3–5 children stay together for 30 days. Psychosocial support is provided to families through home care support services. In daycare centers various services are provided like half-day or full-day pre-school education services, family counseling services, and rehabilitation services.

The Ministry of National Education gives place child rights in curriculumsof schools. The Ministry of National Education mediates the help for education. This assistance includes when schools open and festivals.

Sometimes it assists individuals to meet their needs and food support is provided by the Turkish Women Association. Father support programs are available. Individual counseling services are given for women and there are women- human rights education programs.

Bread is distributed free, food and coal aid are made by the municipality. But if the person getting coal help uses gas, it sells for half the price of coal supplied as aid. Birth help is available. They give place to social action programs like swimming or reading.

Besides these Philanthropist help poor people. University-funded or project supported studies are concentrated in places where the children live. Needy people can get involved in organizations such as associations, foundations easier.

What are the problems related to Child Poverty?

- The child's needs are not met, children/youth marriages are made at the request of the family and these are early marriage.
- Children emulate electronic materials which they can not reach.
- Values change over time. For example, the purpose of the assistance for people with disabilities is reaching a certain number but families have used it in a bad way.
- Children are facing emotional abuse.
- Gender discrimination is made and girls' needs are ignored.
- Recruitment starting age has fallen.
- There are few trainers that speak the language of children who migrate. The poor migrates can not benefit from educational opportunities. Sometimes, the enrollment process is long, enrolled children start in a class which is higher than their actual level.
- Migratory children are used as child laborers.
- Employment opportunities are limited for women. As well, women are reluctant to work sometimes.
- Alarm system does not work well in cases of abuse and neglect. Teachers' knowledge level on this subject is not enough.
- Studies on abuse and neglect of civil society organizations is insufficient.

What are the solution proposals about Child Poverty?
Proposals To Be Made In The Short Term

• Children's minimum requirements should be met with educational aid. – Ministry Of Family And Social Policy
• Training should be given about children's rights. Cooperation should be established between schools and family. – Government
• Incentivized financial aid should be given to support family education (e.g. giving gold for graduates). – Ministry Of Family And Social Policy
• Language education should be emphasized for refugee children. – Ministry of National Education

Proposals To Be Made In The Long Term

• Teacher training should be organized – Ministry of National Education
• Although minimally, family training which starts from pre-natal should be provided – Ministry of National Education and Ministry Of Family And Social Policy
• For getting aid, it should be required to take training – All organisation that help
• Vocational studies should be offered – Ministry Of Family And Social Policy ve Ministry of National Education
• Areas and schools which refugee children settled should be separated and an expert should be provided for each region – Ministry of National Education and Ministry Of Family And Social Policy
• Children should be taught from an early age about violence against women, to be honest, ethical, etc., at school – Ministry of National Education
• Children should be educated about what are the children's rights, when and where they should notify in case of infringement – Ministry of National Education
• Arrangements should be made to work in partnership with educators and social service staff – Ministry Of Family And Social Policy and Ministry of National Education
• Empathy in society should be strengthened – All institutions and organizations

3rd GROUP 2nd SESSION

Strengths of Child Poverty:

- Children learn to stand on their own feet.
- The opportunities are visible.
- Immune system is better developed.
- Having strong empathy - their empathy systems are more powerful.
- Social-emotional development is faster.
- Sense of responsibility and sensitivity, and research skills are more advanced.
- Refugee children have the right to enter the university without examination.

Weaknesses of Child Poverty:

- The risk of being involved in the political game is over.
- Education of children and the mothers do not have enough time.
- Everything that is expected from the state becouse of the lack of solidarity among people.
- Insufficient and unbalanced nutrition are experienced intensely.
- Training needs are not being met.

180

- Lack of stimulus is intense.
- In the family environment, nobody can be the right model.
- Behavior problems are experienced intensely like lack of confidence and jealousy.
- Although there is not a problem in cognitive development, the development of the poor child is much less than their peers. For this reason, a variety of behavior problems are shown.
- Development and behavior problems are experienced.
- There is inequality.
- The result of the ending cooperation in the villages, people drift to loneliest.
- People who get help may be negatively affected socially.
- Especially with children with disabilities the fathers leave the houses.

Opportunities Related to Child Poverty:

- Work to be done in this regard can be realized.
- They are psychologically resistant in the face of events.
- They have features such as easy to take risks.
- Its strengths and weaknesses are well known.
- They do their job in very good shape.
- They are aware of family and sibling bonds.
- Solidarity between them is too much.

Threats Relating to Child Poverty:

- Early marriages are performed.
- Education remains incomplete.
- Working age starts early.
- They feel inadequate about themselves to enter a social environment.
- All kinds of abuse possibilities exist.
- There is a risk involved in terrorist incidents.
- Delinquency rates are intense.
- Vulnerabilities experienced, threats of abuse are intense.
- Due to poverty, child violence, child abuse and neglect can exist.

Appendix 6. Mamak Child Poverty District Action Plan

Action No	ACTION	Agency Or Organization Responsible For The Action	Institutions Or Organizations Concerned With Action	Time to Apply Actions	Explanation Of The Action
1	Resources should be allocated to those who really need and distribution requirements criteria must be evaluated again	Government	The Ministry of Family And Social Policy	Short Term	The criteria for determining the need for state should be revised and updated for the people who need it.
2	Grants must be not only economic support but also psychological and educational	Municipalities Universities Ministries	All organizations that help	Short Term	Poverty should be evaluated and not only financial aspects. All dimensions should be evaluated and accordingly studies should be carried out
3	Grants should be distributed according to the needs and characteristics of the family	All organizations that help	All organizations that help	Short Term	For example not giving sugar to diabetics
4	Soybis system must allow for all aid agencies to use effectively and commonly	All organizations that help	All organizations that help	Short Term	So that everyone can see who gets help and what kind of help.
5	It should be examined that the aid used is for its true aim or not	All organizations that help	All organizations that help	Short Term	Assistance received by people are used based on demand or not
6	Professional persons should conduct a detailed examination of the house	All organizations that help	Experts, Universities	Short Term	Neutral experts or institutions can help with home inspections
7	Trainings for women's employment and training centers for women's employment will be open.	The Ministry of Family and Social Policy The Ministry of Labor and Social Security	The Ministry of Labor and Social Security	Short Term	Those who graduated from these centers should be given job opportunities and so that the female employment rate should be increased

Action No	ACTION	Agency Or Organization Responsible For The Action	Institutions Or Organizations Concerned With Action	Time to Apply Actions	Explanation Of The Action
8	Due to the disposal of basic education in the family, family education should be done through home visits and this education should be expanded.	Municipalities Universities Ministries Prefectures	Municipalities Universities Ministries Prefectures	Short Term	Family support may be provided with different training.
9	Cooperation should be ensured by bringing together disadvantaged groups	All organizations that help	All organizations that help	Short Term	For example, a young woman who gets help can clean someone's home who is very old
10	Community service should be increased	Universities Ministry of National Education	All institutions providing education	Short Term	All levels of education should include community service applications
11	Volunteer work about sharing and solidarity should be made at schools and should be extended	Ministry of National Education	All institutions providing education	Short Term	Activities should be increased for schools in volunteer work, so that a sense of solidarity can be shared
12	Improvement studies should be done about the teachers' professional skills - who are very important for children's life	Ministry of National Education	Teachers in schools	Short Term	Train teachers about where they can receive help and how they can step in
13	It should be provided to schools projects about social services	The Ministry of Family and Social Policy Ministry of National Education	All institutions providing education	Short Term	Examination of students' and parents' profile and Make researchs about social services.

Action No	ACTION	Agency Or Organization Responsible For The Action	Institutions Or Organizations Concerned With Action	Time to Apply Actions	Explanation Of The Action
14	New support policies for the elimination of poverty should be developed	Government the Ministry of Family And Social Policy	Government the Ministry of family and social policy, Ministry of National Education	Long Term	Poverty causes should be identified In-depth policies should be implemented to prevent
15	State-assisted and institutional assistance should be given from one spot	Government Ministry of Family And Social Policy	Government the Ministry of Family And Social Policy, Social Assistance And Solidarity Foundation	Long term	In this way everybody can see who gets what aid
16	Non-governmental organizations and government agencies do not communicate with each other. Therefore it wastes public resources. To prevent this aid should be provided from a single source.	Ministries	All organizations that help	Long term	For more systematic distribution of aid, communication of all aid agencies must be ensured
17	Help should be made for those in need	Ministry of family and social policy prefectures	All organizations that help	Long term	Assistance should be provided according to the needs of people
18	Without distinction, different cultures, income levels and denominations, families should be provided to live together so that they are in contact with each other	Municipalities Ministries	Municipalities Ministries	Long term	In this way, it should be allowed to provide social learning and to model learning

184

Action No	ACTION	Agency Or Organization Responsible For The Action	Institutions Or Organizations Concerned With Action	Time to Apply Actions	Explanation Of The Action
19	Community centers for the training of family should be expanded.	Municipalities the Ministry of Family And Social Policy	Municipalities	Long term	Municipality should give support to these centers with infrastructure and the execution of these institutions must be ensured with staff support from the Ministry of Family and Social Policy
20	Community centers, child-youth centers and centers for street children must be opened and should be expanded	Ministry of family and social policy	Municipalities the Ministry of family and social policy	Long term	Opening such centers should be provided in the neighborhood and areas that children can receive education and social development that can be supported should be extended
21	Access to service centers should be facilitated	Municipalities Ministries	Municipalities	Long term	People, should facilitate the access to service centers like education, health, etc.
22	Giving financial support to the family should be considered a final solution, solution-oriented work should be increased like increasing employment opportunities	Government the Ministry of Labor and Social Security	Ministry of Labor and Social Security	Long term	Improving employment opportunities
23	The labor force participation of the needy should be provided. Family business workshops where they can learn professions should be opened.	Ministries Ministry of Labor and Social Security	Ministries the Ministry of Labor and Social Security	Long term	It should also be allowed to work from home to those who can not work outside the home

185

Action No	ACTION	Agency Or Organization Responsible For The Action	Institutions Or Organizations Concerned With Action	Time to Apply Actions	Explanation Of The Action
24	In addition to the orphanages children's homes system should be extended	Ministry of family and social policy	Orphanages children's homes system	Long term	Children should be supported to live in their home environment
25	Children should be raised with work ethics with well-crafted educational policies	Ministries	Ministry of National Education	Long term	Children will be provided with information about work and work ethics.
26	Free pre-school education institutions should be created in poor neighborhoods. This system should supply their food needs	Ministry of National Education	Pre-school education institutions	Long term	Pre-school education should become compulsory again, the execution of the training should be provided with the family
27	Teachers and professional staff who will work with children should be selected by professionals; "paid teacher system" should be removed	Ministry of National Education	Ministry of National Education	Long term	Teachers should be feel secure about their jobs
28	Children as well as subjects such as mathematics – physics, they should be directed to the job, art or craft based on their ability.	Ministry of National Education	Ministry of National Education	Long term	Educational environment should be created for the provision of education for children in different ways
29	Updates should be made in the education system	Ministry of National Education	Ministry of National Education	Long term	The education system should be updated.

Action No	ACTION	Agency Or Organization Responsible For The Action	Institutions Or Organizations Concerned With Action	Time to Apply Actions	Explanation Of The Action
30	Serious policies should be developed for the training of the family	Ministry Of Family and Social Policy Ministry of National Education	Ministry of National Education the Ministry of family and social policy	Long term	Families should be aware of different topics
31	New regulations system should be done for criminal children and special places should be created for them.	Ministry of Justice	Ministry of Justice	Long term	With detailed studies on the children's crime situation updates must be made
32	Social support systems in the neighborhood should be increased, courses for mothers and fathers, playground for children, pre-school educational institutions, places to spend their spare time for adolescents (library, etc.) should be done and should be expanded	Municipalities	Municipalities Ministry of National Education, the Ministry of family and social policy	Long term	Raising awareness of mothers and children should be provided
33	Loans and lending policies should be changed	Banking regulation and Supervisory Agency	Banking regulation and Supervisory Agency, Banks	Long term	People using income consciously should be provided

187

Appendix 7. Concept Mapping Towards Quantitative Analysis

Concept Map Belongs to Children's Opinion on Child Poverty

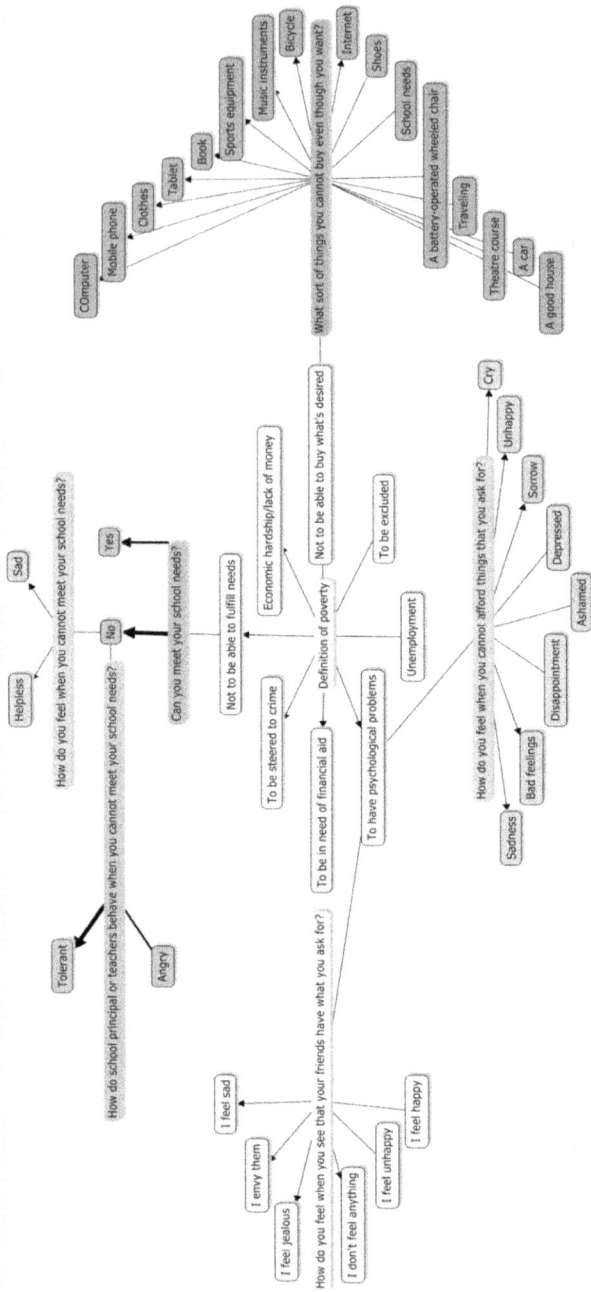

What sort of things you cannot buy even though you want?
- COmputer
- Mobile phone
- Clothes
- Tablet
- Book
- Sports equipment
- Music instruments
- Bicycle
- Internet
- Shoes
- School needs
- A battery-operated wheeled chair
- Traveling
- Theatre course
- A car
- A good house

How do you feel when you cannot meet your school needs?
- Sad
- Helpless

Can you meet your school needs?
- Yes
- No

How do school principal or teachers behave when when you cannot meet your school needs?
- Tolerant
- Angry

Definition of poverty
- Economic hardship/lack of money
- Not to be able to buy what's desired
- To be excluded
- Not to be able to fulfill needs
- To be steered to crime
- To be in need of financial aid
- To have psychological problems
- Unemployment

How do you feel when you cannot afford things that that you ask for?
- Cry
- Unhappy
- Sorrow
- Depressed
- Ashamed
- Disappointment
- Bad feelings
- Sadness

How do you feel when you see that your friends have what you ask for?
- I feel sad
- I envy them
- I feel jealous
- I don't feel anything
- I feel unhappy
- I feel happy

Concept Map Belongs to Parents' Opinion on Child Poverty

Sadness

Unhappiness

Ashamed

Feeling sting of conscience

Feeling broken

Feeling obligation

Crying

How do you feel when you cannot fulfil the needs of your children?

Was there a problem with your child's health due to poverty?
- Yes
- No

Have ever been unable to buy medicine when you got sick?
- Yes
- No

Education level should raise

More justice and equality

State should help

Salaries should be increased

More employment

Helping each other

What can be done to prevent poverty in your opinion?

Unemployment

Economic problems

Diseases

Not to be able to fulfill needs

Definition of Poverty

Something bad

Weariness

Homelessness

To be excluded

Something divine

To have psychological problems

Toys

Mobile phone

Transportation fee

Clothes

School needs

Private room

Social activities

Food

Computer

What kind of needs of your children that you cannot meet?

S/he feels ashamed

S/he gets offended and shows reaction

What's your child's reaction when his/her needs are not fulfilled?

S/he cries, feels sad

S/he makes compare and blame us

Collecting food from bazaar and trashes

Where do you prefer for food shopping?

Bazaar

Buying the cheapest

Peddlers

Market

In an environment with best conditions

In a safer place

What kind of an environment would you like to live in if you had enough income?

In a central, nice neighborhood

In a larger house

Fear of losing spouse

Concern about being alone

Concern about debts

Health problems

What are your concerns about future?

Economical problems

Concern about safety

Unemployment problems

Concern about the future of my children

Has your child ever been unable to continue education due to poverty?
- No
- Yes
- Sometimes

189

www.ingramcontent.com/pod-product-compliance
Lightning Source LLC
Chambersburg PA
CBHW050512280326
41932CB00014B/2294